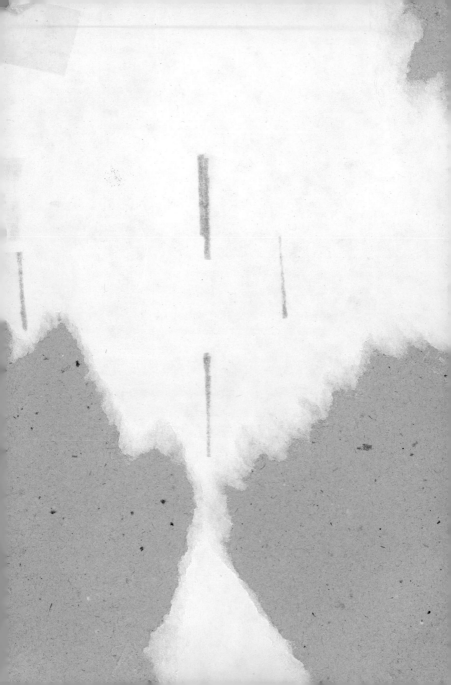

To

Steve and Cindy
with warm regards

Abdul

GROWING WITHIN

The Psychology of Inner Development

Selections from the Works of
SRI AUROBINDO
and
THE MOTHER

Compiled with an Introduction by
A. S. Dalal

SRI AUROBINDO ASHRAM
PONDICHERRY

First Edition: 1992

ISBN 81-7058-315-2

Published by Sri Aurobindo Ashram Publication Department
Printed at Sri Aurobindo Ashram Press, Pondicherry
PRINTED IN INDIA

CONTENTS

Preface ... i

Introduction ... iii

SECTION I

Emergence from Unconsciousness ... 1

SECTION II

Awakening of Consciousness ... 15

SECTION III

Growth of Consciousness: Basic Requisites ... 31
    Aspiration ... 33
    Sincerity ... 38
    Faith ... 41
    The Teaching – Mental Preparation ... 45
    The Teacher ... 52
    Patience and Right Attitude ... 56

SECTION IV

Growth of Consciousness: First Steps and Foundation ... 61
    Purification ... 63
    Concentration ... 68
    Equanimity and Peace ... 72

Section V

Growth of Consciousness: Means and Methods ... 81
  Many Methods ... 83
  Meditation ... 85
  Work ... 93
  Bhakti – Devotion ... 101

Section VI

**Growth of Consciousness: Difficulties
and Pitfalls** ... 107

Section VII

Growth of Consciousness: Inner Experiences ... 125

Section VIII

The Psychic Being and Inner Growth ... 147

Section IX

Reversal of Consciousness – The New Birth ... 163

Glossary ... 177

References ... 187

Index ... 190

It is by a constant inner growth that one can find a constant newness and unfailing interest in life. There is no other satisfying way.

SRI AUROBINDO
(Letters on Yoga, SABCL, Vol. 25, p. 715)

To become ourselves is the one thing to be done; but the true ourselves is that which is within us, and to exceed our outer self of body, life and mind is the condition for this highest being, which is our true and divine being, to become self-revealed and active. It is only by growing within and living within that we can find it....

SRI AUROBINDO
(The Life Divine, SABCL, Vol. 19, p. 1023)

Everything turns around the consciousness, the fact of being or not being conscious. And it is only in the supreme Consciousness that you can attain the perfect expression of yourself.

For the true consciousness is the divine Consciousness. If you cut yourself off from the divine Consciousness, you become absolutely unconscious; that is exactly what has happened. And so, everything there is, the world as it is, your consciousness as it is, things in the state they are in, are the result of this separation of the consciousness and its immediate obscuration.

The minute the individual consciousness is separated from the divine Consciousness, it enters what we call the inconscience, and it is this inconscience that is the cause of all its miseries.

And the conclusion is this, that the true transformation is the transformation of consciousness – all the rest will follow automatically.

THE MOTHER

(Questions and Answers 1956, CWM, Vol. 8, p. 77)

PREFACE

This book aims at shedding some light on the meaning, nature and processes of inner development. Its purpose is to help seekers in understanding and recognising the processes and experiences of inner growth, so as to serve, in some measure, as a guide to those who may not have yet found a personal teacher and mentor.

In order to make the book meaningful to all seekers of growth irrespective of their personal belief systems, the passages included in the compilation have been selected from the viewpoint of the psychological nature of their content, dealing with inner growth as an *experiential* process. Though based on Sri Aurobindo's yoga, the focus is on the universal psychological elements and principles of inner growth, the understanding and validation of which rests on personal experience, introspection and intuition rather than on mental beliefs, although, beliefs can help or hinder the understanding. For this reason, features of the growth process peculiar to Sri Aurobindo's yoga have not been treated in the book, though allusions to such unique features will be found in some of the passages included in the compilation.

Explanations of special terms and concepts contained in the passages will be found in the Glossary at the end of the book. Some of the concepts are also dealt with in the Introduction that follows.

The passages compiled here have been drawn mostly from Sri Aurobindo's letters to his disciples and the Mother's talks to the children of the Ashram. This accounts for their informal style and for the ellipses, pauses, repetitions, etc. which are found in many of the passages.

Apart from the limited exposition of the subject-matter in the Introduction, the psychology of inner development has been presented here in an implicit and non-systematic manner by way of the quoted passages. Though an explicit and systematic exposition, paraphrasing and elaborating upon the contents of the quoted passages, might have been more appealing to the intellect, the original words of a Master have a unique value and can impart far more than a mere intellectual understanding. The receptive reading of words which emanate from such a Master and which are instilled with a consciousness infinitely higher than our own can, besides conveying ideas, effectively serve to elevate the consciousness of the reader, thereby actually inducing inner growth. A moment or two of quiet concentration prior to reading, with an aspiration to be open to the consciousness behind the words, is apt to enhance one's receptivity. It is hoped that the compilation will thus be helpful not only in understanding but also in fostering inner development.

A. S. DALAL

INTRODUCTION

According to Sri Aurobindo, "it is fundamentally an evolution of consciousness that has been taking place in Nature".[1] The inner growth of the human being is simply a continuation of the evolution of consciousness which has hitherto resulted successively in the emergence of Life out of Matter and of Mind out of Life. In other words, consciousness has developed ever higher forms of its manifestation on earth – from the mineral to the plant, to the animal, to man, the mental being. What is called inner growth in this book refers to the evolution of consciousness beyond Mind.

Prior to the appearance of the human or mental being, evolution has been a slow, subconscious process. The emergence of Mind marks the beginning of a *new process of evolution* by which the human being, through a conscious will and aspiration for inner growth, becomes a conscious participant and collaborator in the evolution of consciousness. Thus inner growth is a process of *conscious evolution*. Any system of proven methods for achieving inner growth is yoga; for yoga is "a methodised effort towards self-perfection by the expression of the potentialities latent in the being...."[2] Regarding the two modes of evolution – subconscious evolution through the processes of Nature and conscious evolution through Yoga – Sri Aurobindo writes:

> "All Nature is an attempt at a progressive revelation of the concealed Truth....

1. Sri Aurobindo, *The Life Divine* (SABCL, Vol. 19), p. 846.
2. Sri Aurobindo, *The Synthesis of Yoga* (SABCL, Vol. 20), p. 2.

"But what Nature aims at for the mass in a slow evolution, Yoga effects for the individual by a rapid revolution."[3]

"...their aim is one in the end. The generalisation of Yoga in humanity must be the last victory of Nature over her own delays and concealments. Even as now by the progressive mind in Science she seeks to make all mankind fit for the full development of the mental life, so by Yoga must she inevitably seek to make all mankind fit for the higher evolution, the second birth, the spiritual existence."[4]

Even after the emergence of Mind, the growth of consciousness in the human being continues to be a more or less unconscious process, because the roots of Matter, Life and Mind lie in the Inconscient out of which they have evolved. The first step for emerging out of the primeval unconsciousness is to develop a conscious ego – a separate and independent individuality. So long as an individuality has not been formed, the human being remains an amorphous entity, more or less fused with the unconscious totality of existence. It is by the development of a conscious ego – "...individualisation of being in becoming"[5] – that a person becomes an individual. Ego is the identification of our being with the superficial, outer self made up of the body, the vital nature and the mind. Due to the ego, a certain formation of physical, vital and mental experience is distinguished from the rest of the being and is regarded as the "self". Thus, the ego serves

3. *Ibid.*, p. 24.
4. *Ibid.*
5. Sri Aurobindo, *The Life Divine* (SABCL, Vol. 18), p. 367.

to bring about the emergence from unconsciousness through a progressive consciousness (awareness) of the physical, vital and mental aspects of the being.

Once the separative ego has been adequately developed, evolution of consciousness can be accelerated through growth in a different dimension – that which lies in the transcendence of the ego, liberation from the ignorant identification with one's superficial nature, and the discovery of the true Self. Inner growth, thus, represents a *new dimension of evolution*.

Most of what is today called "personal growth", aimed at by various psychotherapeutic approaches (such as Transactional Analysis, Gestalt Therapy, Rational-Emotive Therapy, etc.) and by the various techniques associated with the Human-Potential Movement (such as Encounter Group, Sensitivity Training, Assertiveness Training, etc.) pertains to what has just been described above as the development of the ego and individuality. On the other hand, inner growth, aimed at by Eastern and Western spiritual approaches (such as Yoga, Zen, Sufism, Christian Mysticism, etc.), consists of "transpersonal" development beyond the ego-state, and represents a total reversal of the normal, ego-bound state of consciousness. It is therefore imperative to distinguish between personal growth and inner growth.[6]

The difference between the presently normal state of consciousness and the more evolved state of consciousness

6. Ken Wilber's book, *No Boundary* (Boston: Shambhala Publications, 1979), which deals with "the major methods of growth and transformation" (Preface), does not make this distinction as indicated by the sub-title of the book: "Eastern and Western Approaches to Personal Growth".

at which inner growth aims is reflected in their contrasting characteristics, some of which are indicated below.

(a) The normal state of consciousness is more or less submerged in unconsciousness: in the normal state, a person is totally unconscious of the deeper and higher levels of the being, and largely unconscious of even the superficial being made up of the body-consciousness, thoughts and feelings. With the inner growth of one's being, there comes an increasing consciousness, for consciousness is the very nature and essence of being.

(b) One of the chief characteristics of the normal state of consciousness is distractibility. The changing impressions and sensations from the outside and the flux of thoughts and feelings from within produce a state of constant distraction. On the other hand, the inner consciousness is centred or concentrated. As the consciousness grows, and one learns to live more and more in the deeper consciousness, one experiences a state of centredness or concentration.

> "The higher consciousness is a concentrated consciousness... not dispersed and rushing about after this or that mental idea or vital desire or physical need as is the ordinary human consciousness – also not invaded by a hundred haphazard thoughts, feelings and impulses, but master of itself, centred and harmonious."[7]

(c) Associated with distraction is another characteristic of the normal state of consciousness, alluded to in the

7. Sri Aurobindo, *Letters on Yoga* (SABCL, Vol. 23), p. 744.

passage just quoted above, namely, dispersion. In the normal state, consciousness is scattered, so to speak, in the superficial parts and movements of the being – physical, vital and mental. As the Mother observes:

> "One throws oneself out all the time; all the time one lives, as it were, outside oneself, in such a superficial sensation that it is almost as though one were outside oneself. As soon as one wants even to observe oneself a little, control oneself a little, simply know what is happening, one is always obliged to draw back or pull towards oneself, to pull inwards something which is constantly like that, on the surface. And it is this surface thing which meets all external contacts, puts you in touch with similar vibrations coming from others. That happens almost outside you. That is the constant dispersal of the ordinary consciousness."[8]

The dispersed nature of the normally prevailing consciousness stands in sharp contrast to the in-gathered and collected nature of the deeper consciousness.

(d) The normal state of consciousness is a state of continual disquiet and agitation due to its constant distractibility and dispersion. As the consciousness grows, one becomes more and more aware of a deeper consciousness which is felt as a substratum of quiet and peace.

> "...Even when it [the inner consciousness] is active, there is felt behind the action or containing it a

8. The Mother, *Questions and Answers 1956* (CWM, Vol. 8), p. 193.

complete quietude or silence. The more one concentrates, the more this quietude and silence increases. That is why there seems to be all quiet
within even though all sorts of things may be taking
place within."[9]

(e) In the normal state, consciousness is involved and
identified with its instruments – the body, the vital nature
and the mind; one feels oneself to *be* the body, thoughts
and feelings. As consciousness evolves, it experiences
itself more and more as detached and separate from the
outer physical, vital and mental nature. Instead of being
identified with the movements of the outer nature, it
observes them as a detached witness – Sakshi, to use a
term of the Gita.

"It [consciousness] can be detached, it can be involved. In the human consciousness it is as a rule
always involved, but it has developed the power of
detaching itself – a thing which the lower creation
seems unable to do. As the consciousness develops,
this power of detachment also develops."[10]

(f) Because of the identification with its instrumental
nature, the ordinary consciousness is afflicted by the
"pairs of contraries"[11] – heat and cold, pleasure and
pain, attraction and repulsion, etc. – which are an inherent characteristic of physical, vital and mental nature.
Ordinarily, therefore, consciousness is in a more or less

9. Sri Aurobindo, *Letters on Yoga* (SABCL, Vol. 23), p. 1000.
10. *Ibid.*, p. 686.
11. Dwandwas (Gita).

constant state of disturbance and disequilibrium. Contrastingly, the higher consciousness is unmoved, fixed or steady – Sthira, to use another term of the Gita. Associated with this quality is Samata – equanimity born of an equal response to the pairs of contraries.

(g) A fundamental characteristic of the normal consciousness is its sense of being a separate self or ego, that is, of being an individual who exists apart from the rest of the universe. On the other hand, the greater consciousness, as described by those who have attained it permanently or experienced it momentarily, is unitary, universal and transpersonal, devoid of separation and division.

> "... the limits of ego, personal mind and body disappear and one becomes aware of a cosmic vastness.... It is not that the ego, the body, the personal mind disappear, but one feels them as only a small part of oneself. One begins to feel others too as part of oneself or varied repetitions of oneself, the same self modified by Nature in other bodies."[12]

The difference, from the viewpoint of yoga, between personal growth and inner growth may be re-stated in

12. Sri Aurobindo, *Letters on Yoga* (SABCL, Vol. 22), p. 316.
Some have spoken of even a still higher state of consciousness, transcending cosmic consciousness, describing it in terms such as these: "... on the other side of the cosmic consciousness there is, attainable to us, a consciousness yet more transcendent, – transcendent not only of the ego, but of the Cosmos itself, – against which the universe seems to stand out like a petty picture against an immeasurable background." Sri Aurobindo, *The Life Divine* (SABCL, Vol. 18), p. 17.

somewhat different words thus: personal growth consists
in the development of the individual as a *human* being,
whereas inner growth, which is the aim of yoga, lies in
transforming and transcending the human state of consciousness.

> "... yoga is not perfection of the human nature as it
> is but a psychic and spiritual transformation of all the
> parts of the being through the action of an inner
> consciousness and then of a higher consciousness
> which works on them, throws out their old move-
> ments or changes them into the image of its own and
> so transmutes lower into higher nature. It is not so
> much the perfection of the intellect as a transcend-
> ence of it, a transformation of the mind, the substi-
> tution of a larger greater principle of knowledge –
> and so with all the rest of the being."[13]

> "The higher perfection is the spiritual perfection,
> integral union with the Divine, identification with
> the Divine, freedom from all the limitations of the
> lower world. That is spiritual perfection, the perfec-
> tion that comes from yoga....
>
> "And the lower perfection is to be able to make
> the human being in his present form and in his body,
> in his relation with all terrestrial things, do the
> utmost he can. This is the case of all great men of
> genius: artistic genius, literary genius, genius in

13. Sri Aurobindo, *Letters on Yoga* (SABCL, Vol. 23), pp. 848-49.
   This was in reply to a seeker who had written that he saw in Sri
Aurobindo "one who achieved through the perfection of the intellect, its
spiritualisation and divination".

organisation, the great rulers, those who have carried physical capacities to their maximum perfection, human development to the limit of its possibilities.... And from every point of view: from the point of view of physical strength, of intellectual realisation, of the physical qualities of energy and courage, of disinterestedness, goodness, charity; all human qualities carried to their utmost limits. That is the lower perfection."[14]

An important point to note in the above-quoted passage is that even moral development – which is often confused with spirituality – is part of growth that belongs to the *human* state; it does not constitute inner growth which aims at a state of the being beyond the human ego-bound state.[15]

Inner growth needs to be distinguished also from what is commonly called the growth of awareness, sought to be fostered by various modern psychological methods and techniques. The term "awareness", as used in modern psychology, has acquired a wide range of meanings and connotations, ranging from the detection of a very weak sensory stimulus, such as a dim light, to the acquisition of insight into the unconscious dynamics which motivate one's actions.[16] From the viewpoint of yoga psychology,

14. The Mother, *Questions and Answers 1957-58* (CWM, Vol. 9), pp. 90-91.

15. However, just as the development of the ego is indispensable for emerging out of unconsciousness, so too moral development, which is one of the highest aspects of human growth, is a necessary step towards a state of consciousness beyond the human.

16. *Vide* Arthur S. Reber, *The Penguin Dictionary of Psychology* (Penguin Books Ltd., 1985), s.v. "awareness" and "awareness, levels of".

what is called awareness in Gestalt therapy and other similar approaches of psychological growth refers to awareness of the outer or surface being, consisting of physical, vital and mental parts of the human make-up; growth of such awareness lies in becoming more and more aware of one's body, feelings, emotions and thoughts. Inner growth, on the other hand, pertains to the progressive awakening and awareness of the inner and higher parts of the being.[17]

In the normal state of consciousness, in which we are identified with the outer being – the body, impulses and feelings, and the mind – we are almost totally unconscious of the inner being and of its constant action on the surface consciousness. We sometimes awaken into the consciousness of the inner being during the sleep of the body, and occasionally bring back to the normal waking consciousness some of our experiences of the inner consciousness during sleep in the form of lucid, symbolic or premonitory dreams, though most of our dreams, which are confused and incoherent, pertain not to the inner consciousness but to the subconscient.[18] We also get glimpses of the inner consciousness through certain images, perceived either spontaneously or during the practice of visualisation, and, in rare cases, through visions or inner voices. In the state of meditation, too, we sometimes become aware of the inner being as a detached, calm and observing consciousness. Apart from these occasional, momentary and fragmentary experiences, the inner being

17. See "Being" in the Glossary at the end of the book for an explanation of the terms.

18. The subconscient is called the unconscious in modern psychology.

is shut out from the outer by the thick wall or veil of the normal, surface consciousness. The process of inner growth consists in the gradual breaking down of the wall or the lifting of the veil, and awakening to the consciousness of the inner being. As Sri Aurobindo writes:

"There are always two different consciousnesses in the human being, one outward in which he ordinarily lives, the other inward and concealed of which he knows nothing. When one does sadhana, the inner consciousness begins to open and one is able to go inside and have all kinds of experiences there. As the sadhana progresses, one begins to live more and more in this inner being and the outer becomes more and more superficial. At first the inner consciousness seems to be the dream and the outer the waking reality. Afterwards the inner consciousness becomes the reality and the outer is felt by many as a dream or delusion, or else as something superficial and external."[19]

A salient aspect of Sri Aurobindo's yoga pertaining to the psychology of inner growth is its view of the inner and higher planes of consciousness as dynamic forces. Though hidden from the outer surface consciousness, the inner and higher parts of the being exercise on the surface parts of the being a constant influence and pressure, pushing towards the evolution and growth of consciousness. Alluding to the "decisive part played by the higher planes [of consciousness] in the earth-evolution"[20], Sri Aurobindo writes:

19. Sri Aurobindo, *Letters on Yoga* (SABCL, Vol. 22), p. 307.
20. Sri Aurobindo, *The Life Divine* (SABCL, Vol. 19), p. 801.

"Our development takes place very largely by their superior but hidden action upon the earth-plane. All is contained in the inconscient or the subconscient, but in potentiality; it is the action from above that helps to compel an emergence. A continuance of that action is necessary to shape and determine the progression of the mental and vital forms which our evolution takes in material nature; for these progressive movements cannot find their full momentum or sufficiently develop their implications against the resistance[21] of an inconscient or inert and ignorant material Nature except by a constant though occult resort to higher supraphysical forces of their own character. This resort, the action of this veiled alliance, takes place principally in our subliminal being and not on the surface: it is from there that the active power of our consciousness emerges, and all that it realises it sends back constantly into the subliminal being to be stored up, developed and re-emerge in stronger forms hereafter. This interaction of our larger hidden being and our surface personality is the main secret of the rapid development that operates in man once he has passed beyond the lower stages of Mind immersed in Matter."[22]

21. The psychoanalytical concept of resistance is a central concept in Sri Aurobindo's yoga psychology as well. In psychoanalysis, it is regarded as caused by unconscious factors, and consists in the opposition to making what is unconscious conscious in the analytical process. From Sri Aurobindo's metapsychological viewpoint, resistance is a force of the Inconscient which opposes the growth and transformation of consciousness.

22. Sri Aurobindo, *The Life Divine* (SABCL, Vol. 19), pp. 801-02.

Regarding the influence of the inner planes of consciousness on the outer life of the individual, Sri Aurobindo states:

> "It is a mistake to think that we live physically only, with the outer mind and life. We are all the time living and acting on other planes of consciousness, meeting others there and acting upon them, and what we do and feel and think there, the forces we gather, the results we prepare have an incalculable importance and effect, unknown to us, upon our outer life. Not all of it comes through, and what comes through takes another form in the physical – though sometimes there is an exact correspondence; but this little is at the basis of our outward existence. All that we become and do and bear in the physical life is prepared behind the veil within us."[23]

> "It [the inner being] is, according to our psychology, connected with the small outer personality by certain centres of consciousness of which we become aware by yoga. Only a little of the inner being escapes through these centres into the outer life, but that little is the best part of ourselves and responsible for our art, poetry, philosophy, ideals, religious aspirations, efforts at knowledge and perfection."[24]

To sum up, the inner growth of the individual, like the evolution of the universe, is the process by which the Supreme Consciousness – the Truth of Existence or the

23. Sri Aurobindo, *Letters on Yoga* (SABCL, Vol. 23), pp. 993-94.
24. Sri Aurobindo, *Letters on Yoga* (SABCL, Vol. 24), pp. 1164-65.

Reality of Being, immersed in the Inconscience of Matter through a prior process of involution, manifests itself in progressively higher states of its being due to the evolutionary thrust inherent in it.

In Sri Aurobindo's yoga, the Supreme Consciousness, Truth or Reality is spoken of as the Divine, "the Supreme Being from whom all have come and in whom all are".[25] The portion of the Divine Consciousness which develops in the process of evolution is called the soul or the psychic essence. It grows and becomes a distinct individuality, referred to as the psychic being. It is through the psychic being that the evolutionary dynamism inherent in the Supreme Consciousness brings about the inner growth of the individual. Explaining the nature of the psychic entity and the process of its evolution Sri Aurobindo writes:

> "At the beginning the soul in Nature, the psychic entity, whose unfolding is the first step towards a spiritual change, is an entirely veiled part of us, although it is that by which we exist and persist as individual beings in Nature. The other parts of our natural composition are not only mutable but perishable; but the psychic entity in us persists and is fundamentally the same always; it contains all essential possibilities of our manifestation but is not constituted by them; it is not limited by what it manifests, not contained by the incomplete forms of the manifestation, not tarnished by the imperfections and impurities, the defects and depravations of the surface being. It is an ever-pure flame of the divinity in things and nothing that comes to it,

25. Sri Aurobindo, *Letters on Yoga* (SABCL, Vol. 23), p. 1081.

nothing that enters into our experience can pollute its purity or extinguish the flame. The spiritual stuff is immaculate and luminous and, because it is perfectly luminous, it is immediately, intimately, directly aware of truth of being and truth of nature; it is deeply conscious of truth and good and beauty because truth and good and beauty are akin to its own native character, forms of something that is inherent in its own substance. It is aware also of all that contradicts these things, of all that deviates from its own native character, of falsehood and evil and the ugly and the unseemly; but it does not become these things nor is it touched or changed by these opposites of itself which so powerfully affect its outer instrumentation of mind, life and body....

"As the evolution proceeds, Nature begins slowly and tentatively to manifest our occult parts; she leads us to look more and more within ourselves or sets out to initiate more clearly recognisable intimations and formations of them on the surface. The soul in us, the psychic principle, has already begun to take secret form ; it puts forward and develops a soul-personality, a distinct psychic being to represent it."[26]

"The psychic part of us is something that comes direct from the Divine and is in touch with the Divine. In its origin it is the nucleus pregnant with divine possibilities that supports this lower triple manifestation of mind, life and body. There is this

26. Sri Aurobindo, *The Life Divine* (SABCL, Vol. 19), pp. 891-92, 893.

divine element in all living beings, but it stands
behind the ordinary consciousness, is not at first
developed and, even when developed, is not always
or often in the front; it expresses itself, so far as the
imperfection of the instruments allows, by their
means and under their limitations. It grows in the
consciousness by Godward experience, gaining
strength every time there is a higher movement in
us, and, finally, by the accumulation of these deeper
and higher movements, there is developed a psychic
individuality, – that which we call usually the psychic
being."[27]

Numerous are the paths that have been discovered for
achieving inner growth and realising the Truth. The
various psychological paths may be classified into three
broad types, corresponding to the three basic psychological aspects of the human make-up: the Path of Knowledge, corresponding to the cognitive or thinking aspect;
the Path of Devotion, related to the affective or emotional
side of human nature; and the Path of Works or Action,
based on man's conative aspect which has to do with
striving and willing. Almost all paths contain elements of
each of the three broad types just mentioned, though one
particular type element – Knowledge, Devotion, or
Works – may predominate. The seeker is drawn to one
path or another depending on what predominates in one's
psychological make-up. Regarding the best path to follow,
the rule is contained in the celebrated words of the Gita:

"Better is Swadharma – the law of one's own being –

27. Sri Aurobindo, *Letters on Yoga* (SABCL, Vol. 22), p. 288.

even though itself faulty, than an alien law well wrought out; death in one's own law of being is better, perilous it is to follow a law foreign to one's own nature." (III:35)

Though the different paths vary greatly in their methods and processes, certain elements are common to them all. One such universal element is a certain preliminary cleansing or purification of the outer nature, consisting of the physical, vital and mental consciousness. An attempt to enter into the inner consciousness without adequately ridding the outer consciousness of its turbidity is apt to fail; if at all one succeeds in some measure, one is most likely to be confused, misled or overwhelmed by the experiences of the inner consciousness without a sufficient foundation of a calm purity in the outer being.

A second element common to all paths of inner growth consists in developing an in-gathered attitude, a state of inner concentration which progressively replaces the state of outer dispersion characteristic of the normal consciousness. The in-gathered state is most often sought to be inculcated through the practice of meditation. That is why, to many people, the spiritual life is almost synonymous with the practice of meditation: "...when they think of the spiritual life, they immediately think of meditation".[28] Such an attitude tends to lead to a false compartmentalisation of life, a division and antagonism between the spiritual life and the ordinary life. However, true spirituality lies, not in any form of practice, but in living in a certain *state of consciousness* pervading *all* life

28. The Mother, *Questions and Answers 1957-58* (CWM, Vol. 9), p. 88.

and activities. Meditation – in the sense of a set practice – is not indispensable for cultivating such a spiritual state of inner concentration; action and work done with the right consciousness also produce a state of meditation.

The form in which one experiences and realises the Truth depends on the nature of the path one follows. Thus the paths of the Adwaitin and the Buddhist lead to the experience of Nirvana and the realisation of the Truth as an impersonal Principle – an Impersonal Absolute Existence (Adwaita) or an Impersonal Absolute Non-Existence (Buddhism). On the other hand, the paths based on self-consecration through works and action, such as the path of the Gita, and the paths of devotion and prayer, such as that of the Christian mystics, lead to the experience of the Truth as a Personal Being, Ishwara, the Lord. An integral approach, states Sri Aurobindo, leads to the realisation of the Truth as both personal and impersonal. He writes:

> "...if we carry up our heart as well as our reasoning mind to the Highest, we shall find that we can reach it through the absolute Person as well as through an absolute impersonality.... [In its universal aspect] too we meet him in various forms of divine personality; in formulations of quality which variously express him to us in his nature; in infinite quality, the Anantaguna; in the divine Person who expresses himself through infinite quality; in absolute impersonality, an absolute existence or an absolute non-existence, which is yet all the time the unexpressed Absolute of this divine Person, this conscious Being who manifests himself through us and through the universe."[29]

29. Sri Aurobindo, *The Synthesis of Yoga* (SABCL, Vol. 21), p. 560.

Whatever the path followed, the process of inner growth involves a transformation of the normal state of consciousness, a progressive awakening of inner and higher states of being, culminating in a total reversal of consciousness, a new birth.

One feature of the reversal of consciousness – which gives it the appearance of a sudden revolution rather than a gradual change – is that it involves a process similar to what has been called "unconscious incubation". The term "incubation" has been used in psychology to denote "a period of time during which no conscious effort is made to solve a problem but which terminates with the solution".[30] (Hence the advice to "sleep" over an insoluble problem, waiting for the solution to emerge.) A somewhat similar phenomenon is involved in the reversal of consciousness. It is a sudden happening, preceded by a more or less long period of preparation which takes place behind the veil of the surface consciousness and of which the seeker is therefore unaware.

> "For a long time you have the impression that nothing is happening, that your consciousness is the same as usual, and, if you have an intense aspiration, you even feel a resistance, as though you were knocking against a wall which does not yield. But when you are ready within, a last effort – the pecking in the shell of the being – and everything opens and you are projected into another consciousness."[31]

A. S. DALAL

30. Arthur S. Reber, *The Penguin Dictionary of Psychology* (Penguin Books Ltd., 1985), s.v. "incubation".

31. The Mother, *Questions and Answers 1950-51* (CWM, Vol. 4), pp. 18-19.

I

EMERGENCE FROM UNCONSCIOUSNESS

Here everything is shut up from the first in the violently working inconscient sleep of material force; therefore the whole aim of any material becoming must be the waking of consciousness out of the inconscient; the whole consummation of a material becoming must be the removal of the veil of Matter and the luminous revelation of the entirely self-conscient Being to its own imprisoned soul in the becoming.

SRI AUROBINDO

... the appearance of human mind and body on the earth marks a crucial step, a decisive change in the course and process of the evolution; it is not merely a continuation of the old lines. Up till this advent of a developed thinking mind in Matter evolution had been effected, not by the self-aware aspiration, intention, will or seeking of the living being, but subconsciously or subliminally by the automatic operation of Nature. This was so because the evolution began from the Inconscience and the secret Consciousness had not emerged sufficiently from it to operate through the self-aware participating individual will of its living creature. But in man the necessary change has been made, – the being has become awake and aware of himself; there has been made manifest in Mind its will to develop, to grow in knowledge, to deepen the inner and widen the outer existence, to increase the capacities of the nature.... In him, then, the substitution of a conscious for a subconscious evolution has become conceivable and practicable, and it may well be concluded that the aspiration, the urge, the persistent endeavour in him is a sure sign of Nature's will for a higher way to fulfilment, the emergence of a greater status.

SRI AUROBINDO

EMERGENCE FROM UNCONSCIOUSNESS

People usually do things so automatically and spontaneously, without watching themselves doing them, that if
they were to ask themselves how it comes about, they
would require some time before the process becomes
conscious to them. You are so used to living that you don't
even know how it happens. All the gestures and movements of life are made spontaneously, automatically,
almost unconsciously, in a semi-conscious state, and one
doesn't even realise this very simple fact that in order to
do something, one must first know what one is going to do
and then must want to do it. It is only when something
goes wrong with one of these elements – for instance, the
ability to make a plan in one's mind and the ability to
carry out this plan – when these two begin to go wrong,
one starts worrying about whether one's being is in good
order. For example, if one morning on waking up in bed
you did not know or remember that you had to get up,
wash and dress, have your breakfast, do this and that, you
would say to yourself, "Why, what's the matter? Something is wrong – I don't know what I ought to do any
more; something must be out of order."

And if, later, knowing what you have to do – you must
get up, go for your bath, dress – you know you have to do
it but you can't do it: there is something, the stimulus of
the will, which is no longer working, has no effect on the
body; then once again you begin to feel anxious, you say,
"Well, well, could I be ill by any chance?"

Otherwise you are not even aware that the whole of life
is like that. It seems quite natural to you, it is "like that".
That means that you act in a way which is hardly semi-

conscious; it is automatic, it is a kind of spontaneous habit and you don't watch what you are doing. And so, if you want to have some control over your movements, the first thing is to know what is happening.

And in fact, this perhaps is the reason why things don't always go well. For if they went according to a normal, usual rhythm, one would never be conscious of what one is doing; one would do it by habit, automatically, spontaneously, without thinking, and would not watch what one is doing, and so one would never be able to acquire self-mastery. It would be "something", a vague consciousness in the background expressing itself without your even watching what you are doing, and which would make you act; and then if there came along some strange or unknown current of force, it could make you do anything at all, without your even noticing the process by which it makes you act. And in fact that is what does happen.

It is only when one is fully conscious of the process, when one knows how life works, the movement of life and the process of life, that one can begin to have control; otherwise at first one doesn't even think at all of having any control; but if unpleasant things occur, if, for instance, you do something which has unfortunate consequences and you tell yourself, "Oh! but I should stop doing that", then, at that moment, you realise that there is a whole technique of "how to live" which is necessary to be able to control your life! Otherwise one is a kind of more or less coordinated medley of actions and reactions, of movements and impulses, and one doesn't know at all how things happen. This is what is developed in the being by shocks, frictions, all the apparent disorders of life, and what forms the consciousness in very small children. A small child is altogether unconscious, and only gradually, very gradually, does he begin to grow aware of things. But unless they take special care, people live almost their whole life without even knowing how they do it! They are not aware of it.

So anything at all can happen.

But that is the *very first little step* towards becoming conscious of oneself in the material world.

You have vague thoughts and feelings, don't you, which develop more or less logically in the being – rather less than more – then you have a faint impression of that; and again, when you get burnt, you realise that something is wrong, when you fall and hurt yourself, you realise that something is wrong: it begins to make you reflect that you must pay attention to this and that, so as not to fall, not to burn yourself, not to cut yourself.... It dawns on you gradually with external experience, external contacts But otherwise one is a half-conscious mass which moves without even knowing why or how.

This is the very small beginning of the emergence from the primary state of unconsciousness.

THE MOTHER

One lives by a kind of habit which is barely half-conscious – one lives, does not even objectify what one does, why one does it, how one does it. One does it by habit. All those who are born in a certain environment, a certain country, automatically take the habits of that environment, not only material habits but habits of thought, habits of feeling and habits of acting. They do it without watching themselves doing it, quite naturally, and if someone points this out to them they are astonished.

As a matter of fact, one has the habit of sleeping, speaking, eating, moving and one does all this as something quite natural, without wondering why or how.... And many other things. All the time one does things automatically, by force of habit, one does not watch oneself. And so, when one lives in a particular society, one automatically does what is normally done in that society. And if somebody begins to watch himself acting, watch himself feeling and thinking, he looks like a kind of phenomenal monster compared with the environment he lives in.

Therefore, individuality is not at all the rule, it is an exception, and if you do not have that sort of bag, a particular form which is your outer body and your appearance, you could hardly be distinguished from one another.

Individuality is a conquest. And, as Sri Aurobindo says here, this first conquest is only a first stage, and once you have realised within you something like a personal independent and conscious being, then what you have to do is to break the form and go farther. For example, if you want to progress mentally, you must break all your mental forms, all your mental constructions to be able to make new ones. So, to begin with, a tremendous labour is required to individualise oneself, and afterwards one must demolish all that has been done in order to progress.

THE MOTHER

"When we have passed beyond enjoyings, then we shall have Bliss. Desire was the helper; Desire is the bar.

*"When we have passed beyond individualsing, then
we shall be real Persons. Ego was the helper; Ego is
the bar.
"When we have passed beyond humanity, then we
shall be the Man. The Animal was the helper; the
Animal is the bar."*

Sri Aurobindo
(*Thoughts and Glimpses*, SABCL, Vol. 16, p. 377)

It is the same principle expressed in all the activities or
aspects of the being.... It is obvious that in order to come
out of the state of the orginal inconscience desire was
indispensable, for without desire there would have been
no awakening to activity. But once you are *born* into
consciousness, this very desire which helped you to come
out of the inconscience prevents you from liberating
yourself from the bonds of matter and rising to a higher
consciousness.

It is the same thing for the ego, the self. In order to pass
on to a higher plane, one must first exist; and to exist one
must become a conscious, separate individual, and to
become a conscious separate individual, the ego is indispensable, otherwise one remains mingled with all that lies
around us. But once the individuality is formed, if one
wants to rise to a higher level and live a spiritual life, if
one wants even to become simply a higher type of man,
the limitations of the ego are the worst obstacles, and the
ego must be surpassed in order to enter the true consciousness.

And indeed, for the ordinary elementary life of man, all
the qualities belonging to the animal nature, especially

those of the body, were indispensable, otherwise man would not have existed. But when man has become a conscious, mental being, everything that binds him to his animal origin necessarily becomes a hindrance to progress and to the liberation of the being.

So, for everyone – except for those who are born free, and this is obviously very rare – for everyone this state of reason, of effort, desire, individualisation and solid physical balance in accordance with the ordinary mode of living is indispensable to begin with, until the time one becomes a conscious being, when one must give up all these things in order to become a spiritual being.

THE MOTHER

When can one say that one is conscious?

That is always a relative question. One is never altogether unconscious and one is never completely conscious. It is a progressive state.

But a time comes when instead of doing things automatically, impelled by a consciousness and force of which one is quite unaware – a time comes when one can observe what goes on in oneself, study one's movements, find their causes, and at the same time begin to exercise a control first over what goes on within us, then on the influence cast on us from outside which makes us act, in the beginning altogether unconsciously and almost involuntarily, but gradually more and more consciously; and the will can wake up and react. Then at that moment, the moment there is a conscious will capable of reacting, one may say, "I have become conscious." This does not mean that it is a total and perfect consciousness, it means that it is a beginning: for example, when one is able to observe all the reactions in one's being and to have a certain control over them, to let those one approves of have play, and to control, stop, annul those one doesn't approve of.

Besides, you must become aware within of something like a goal or a purpose or an ideal you want to realise; something other than the mere instinct which impels you to live without your knowing why or how. At that time you may say you are conscious, but it doesn't mean you are perfectly conscious. And moreover, this perfection is so progressive that I believe nobody can say he is perfectly conscious; he is on the way to becoming perfectly conscious, but he isn't yet.

THE MOTHER

What part has sorrow played in the evolution of humanity?

Sorrow, desire, suffering, ambition and every other similar reaction in the feelings and sensations have all contributed to make consciousness emerge from the inconscience and to awaken this consciousness to the will for progress.

THE MOTHER

"Man seeks at first blindly and does not even know that he is seeking his divine self; for he starts from the obscurity of material Nature and even when he begins to see, he is long blinded by the light that is increasing in him."

SRI AUROBINDO
(*Thoughts and Glimpses*, SABCL, Vol. 16, p. 382)

How is it that one seeks something and yet does not know that one is seeking?

There are so many things you think, feel, want, even do, without knowing it. Are you fully conscious of yourself and of all that goes on in you? – Not at all! If, for example, suddenly, without your expecting it, at a certain moment I ask you: "What are you thinking about?" your reply , ninety-nine times out of a hundred, will be: "I don't know." And if in the same way I ask another question like this: "What do you want?" you will also say: "I don't know." And "What do you feel?" – "I don't know." It is only to those who are used to observing themselves, watching how they live, who are concentrated upon this need to know what is going on in them, that one can ask a precise question like this, and only they can immediately reply. In some instances in life, yes, one is absorbed in what one feels, thinks, wants, and then one can say, "Yes, I want that, I am thinking of that, I experience that", but these are only moments of existence, not the whole time.

Haven't you noticed that? No?

Well, to find out what one truly is, to find out why one is on earth, what is the purpose of physical existence, of this presence on earth, of this formation, this existence... the vast majority of people live without asking themselves this even once! Only a small *élite* ask themselves this question with interest, and fewer still start working to get the answer. For, unless one is fortunate enough to come across someone who knows it, it is not such an easy thing to find. Suppose, for instance, that there had never come to your hands a book of Sri Aurobindo's or of any of the writers or philosophers or sages who have dedicated their lives to this quest; if you were in the ordinary world, as millions of people are in the ordinary world, who have never heard of anything, except at times – and not always nowadays, even quite rarely – of some gods and a certain form of religion which is more a habit than a faith and, which, besides, rarely tells you why you are on earth.... Then, one doesn't even think of thinking about it. One lives from day to day the events of each day. When one is very young, one thinks of playing, eating, and a little later of learning, and after that one thinks of all the circumstances of life. But to put this problem to oneself, to confront this problem and ask oneself: "But after all, *why* am I here?" How many do that? There are people to whom this idea comes only when they are facing a catastrophe. When they see someone whom they love die or when they find themselves in particularly painful and difficult circumstances, they turn back upon themselves, if they are sufficiently intelligent, and ask themselves: "But really, what is this tragedy we are living, and what's the use of it and what is its purpose?"

And only at that moment does one begin the search to know.

And it is only when one has found, you see, found what he says, found that one has a divine Self and that consequently one must seek to know this divine Self.... This comes much later, and yet, in spite of everything, from the very moment of birth in a physical body, there is in the being, in its depths, this psychic presence which pushes the whole being towards this fulfilment. But who knows it and recognises it, this psychic being? That too comes only in special circumstances, and unfortunately, most of the time these have to be painful circumstances, otherwise one goes on living unthinkingly. And in the depths of one's being is this psychic being which seeks, seeks, seeks to awaken the consciousness and re-establish the union. One knows nothing about it....

Essentially, it is only when one has become aware of one's soul, has been identified with one's psychic being that one can see in a single flash the picture of one's individual development through the ages. Then indeed one begins to know...but not before. Then, indeed, I assure you it becomes very interesting. It changes one's position in life.

There is such a great difference between feeling vaguely, having a hesitant impression of something, of a force, a movement, an impulse, an attraction, of something which drives you in life – but it is still so vague, so uncertain, it is hazy – there is such a difference between this and having a clear vision, an exact perception, a total understanding of the meaning of one's life. And only then does one begin to see things as they are, not before. Only then can one follow the thread of one's destiny and clearly see the goal and the way to reach it. But that happens only through successive inner awakenings, like doors opening suddenly on new horizons – truly, a new birth into a truer, deeper, more lasting consciousness.

Until then you live in a cloud, gropingly, under the weight of a destiny which at times crushes you, gives you the feeling of having been made in a certain way and being unable to do anything about it. You are under the burden of an existence which weighs you down, makes you crawl on the ground instead of rising above and seeing all the threads, the guiding threads, the threads which bind different things into a single movement of progression towards a realisation that grows clear.

One must spring up out of this half-consciousness which is usually considered quite natural – this is your "normal" way of being and you do not even draw back from it sufficiently to be able to see and wonder at this incertitude, this lack of precision; while, on the contrary, to know that one is seeking and to seek consciously, deliberately, *steadfastly* and methodically, this indeed is the exceptional, almost "abnormal" condition. And yet only in this way does one begin to truly live.

THE MOTHER

What is one to do to prepare oneself for the Yoga?

To be conscious, first of all. We are conscious of only an insignificant portion of our being; for the most part we are unconscious. It is this unconsciousness that keeps us down to our unregenerate nature and prevents change and transformation in it. It is through unconsciousness that the undivine forces enter into us and make us their slaves. You are to be conscious of yourself, you must awake to your nature and movements, you must know why and how you do things or feel or think them; you must understand your motives and impulses, the forces, hidden and apparent, that move you; in fact, you must, as it were, take to pieces the entire machinery of your being. Once you are conscious, it means that you can distinguish and sift things, you can see which are the forces that pull you down and which help you on.

THE MOTHER

To be individualised in a collectivity, one must be absolutely conscious of oneself... the Self which is above all intermixture,... the Truth of your being. And as long as you are not conscious of the Truth of your being, you are moved by all kinds of things, without taking any note of it at all. Collective thought, collective suggestions are a formidable influence which act constantly on individual thought.... To escape this there is but one means: to become conscious of oneself, more and more conscious....

THE MOTHER

In the crowd the individual loses his inner direction and becomes a cell of the mass-body moved by the collective will or idea or the mass-impulse. He has to stand apart, affirm his separate reality in the whole, his own mind emerging from the common mentality, his own life distinguishing itself in the common life-uniformity, even as his body has developed something unique and recognisable in the common physicality.... Nature invented the ego that the individual might disengage himself from the inconscience or subconscience of the mass and become an independent living mind, life-power, soul, spirit, coordinating himself with the world around him but not drowned in it.... For the individual is indeed part of the cosmic being, but he is also something more, he is a soul that has descended from the Transcendence. This he cannot manifest at once, because he is too near to the cosmic Inconscience, not near enough to the original Superconscience; he has to find himself as the mental and vital ego before he can find himself as the soul or spirit.

SRI AUROBINDO

II

AWAKENING OF CONSCIOUSNESS

... spirituality is not a high intellectuality, not idealism, not an ethical turn of mind or moral purity and austerity, not religiosity or an ardent and exalted emotional fervour, not even a compound of all these excellent things; a mental belief, creed or faith, an emotional aspiration, a regulation of conduct according to a religious or ethical formula are not spiritual achievement and experience. These things are of considerable value to mind and life; they are of value to the spiritual evolution itself as preparatory movements disciplining, purifying or giving a suitable form to the nature; but they still belong to the mental evolution, – the beginning of a spiritual realisation, experience, change is not yet there. Spirituality is in its essence an awakening to the inner reality of our being, to a spirit, self, soul which is other than our mind, life and body, an inner aspiration to know, to feel, to be that, to enter into contact with the greater Reality beyond and pervading the universe which inhabits also our own being, to be in communion with It and union with It, and a turning, a conversion, a transformation of our whole being as a result of the aspiration, the contact, the union, a growth or waking into a new becoming or new being, a new self, a new nature.

SRI AUROBINDO

The greater and greater awakening of consciousness and its climb to a higher and higher level and a wider extent of its vision and action is the condition of our progress towards that supreme and total perfection which is the aim of our existence.

SRI AUROBINDO

AWAKENING OF CONSCIOUSNESS

All Yoga is in its nature a new birth; it is a birth out of the ordinary, the mentalised material life of man into a higher spiritual consciousness and a greater and diviner being. No Yoga can be successfully undertaken and followed unless there is a strong awakening to the necessity of that larger spiritual existence. The soul that is called to this deep and vast change, may arrive in different ways to the initial departure. It may come to it by its own natural development which has been leading it unconsciously towards the awakening; it may reach it through the influence of a religion or the attraction of a philosophy; it may approach it by a slow illumination or leap to it by a sudden touch or shock; it may be pushed or led to it by the pressure of outward circumstances or by an inward necessity, by a single word that breaks the seals of the mind or by long reflection, by the distant example of one who has trod the path or by contact and daily influence. According to the nature and the circumstances the call will come.

But in whatever way it comes, there must be a decision of the mind and the will and, as its result, a complete and effective self-consecration. The acceptance of a new spiritual idea-force and upward orientation in the being, an illumination, a turning or conversion seized on by the will and the heart's aspiration, – this is the momentous act which contains as in a seed all the results that the Yoga has to give. The mere idea or intellectual seeking of something higher beyond, however strongly grasped by the mind's interest, is ineffective unless it is seized on by the heart as the one thing desirable and by the will as the one thing to be done. For truth of the Spirit has not to be merely thought but to be lived, and to live it demands a unified single-mindedness of the being; so great a change as is contemplated by the Yoga is not to be effected by a divided will or by a small portion of the energy or by a hesitating mind. He who seeks the Divine must consecrate himself to God and to God only.

If the change comes suddenly and decisively by an over-powering influence, there is no further essential or lasting difficulty. The choice follows upon the thought, or is simultaneous with it, and the self-consecration follows upon the choice. The feet are already set upon the path, even if they seem at first to wander uncertainly and even though the path itself may be only obscurely seen and the knowledge of the goal may be imperfect. The secret Teacher, the inner Guide is already at work, though he may not yet manifest himself or may not yet appear in the person of his human representative. Whatever difficulties and hesitations may ensue, they cannot eventually prevail against the power of the experience that has turned the current of the life. The call, once decisive, stands; the thing that has been born cannot eventually be stifled. Even if the force of circumstances prevents a regular pursuit or a full practical self-consecration from the first, still the mind has taken its bent and persists and returns with an ever-increasing effect upon its leading preoccupation. There is an ineluctable persistence of the inner being, and against it, circumstances are in the end power-less, and no weakness in the nature can for long be an obstacle.

But this is not always the manner of the commence-ment. The Sadhaka is often led gradually and there is a long space between the first turning of the mind and the full assent of the nature to the thing towards which it turns. There may at first be only a vivid intellectual interest, a forcible attraction towards the idea and some imperfect form of practice. Or perhaps there is an effort not favoured by the whole nature, a decision or a turn imposed by an intellectual influence or dictated by personal affection and admiration for someone who is himself consecrated and devoted to the Highest. In such cases, a long period of preparation may be necessary before there comes the irrevocable consecration; and in some instances it may not come. There may be some advance, there may be a strong effort, even much purification and many experiences other than those that are central or supreme; but the life will either be spent in preparation or, a certain stage having been reached, the mind pushed by an insufficient driving-force may rest content at the limit of the effort possible to it. Or there may even be a recoil to the lower life, – what is called in the ordinary parlance of Yoga a fall from the path. This lapse happens because there is a defect at the very centre. The intellect has been interested, the heart attracted, the will has strung itself to the effort, but the whole nature has not been taken captive by the Divine. It has only acquiesced in the interest, the attraction or the endeavour. There has been an experiment, perhaps even an eager experiment, but not a total self-giving to an imperative need of the soul or to an unforsakable ideal. Even such imperfect Yoga has not been wasted; for no upward effort is made in vain. Even if it fails in the present or arrives only at some preparatory stage or preliminary realisation, it has yet determined the soul's future.

But if we desire to make the most of the opportunity that this life gives us, if we wish to respond adequately to the call we have received and to attain to the goal we have glimpsed, not merely advance a little towards it, it is essential that there should be an entire self-giving. The secret of success in Yoga is to regard it not as one of the aims to be pursued in life, but as the whole of life.

Sri Aurobindo

It is enough to have had once one minute of aspiration and a will even if it be very fugitive, to become conscious of the Divine, to realise the Divine, for it to flash like lightning through the whole being – there are even cells of the body which respond. This is not visible all at once, but there is a response everywhere. And it is by slowly, carefully, putting together all these parts which have responded, though it be but once, that one can build up something which will be coherent and organised, and which will permit one's action to continue with will, sincerity and perseverance.

Even a fleeting idea in a child, at a certain moment in its childhood when the psychic being is most in front, if it succeeds in penetrating through the outer consciousness and giving the child just an impression of something beautiful which must be realised, it creates a little nucleus and upon this you build your action. There is a vast mass of humanity to whom one would never say, "You must realise the Divine" or "Do yoga to find the Divine." If you observe well you will see that it is a tiny minority to whom this can be said. It means that this minority of beings is "prepared" to do yoga, it is that. It is that there has been a beginning of realisation – a beginning is enough.

THE MOTHER

How can one become aware of the central will?

First of all one must become aware of what is highest, most true, most universal and eternal in one's consciousness.

This is learnt gradually. One learns to discern among one's ordinary, external movements and the different gradations of the movements of one's inner consciousness. And if one continues to do this with a certain persistence, one realises what it is that puts this highest part of one's being into motion, which represents the ideal of the being. There is no other way. Sometimes this awakens through reading something, sometimes through a conversation, sometimes through a more or less dramatic, that is, unexpected event, which gives you a shock, shakes you up, brings you out of your usual little rut. Sometimes when you are in very great danger, suddenly you feel as though you are above yourself and beyond your small habitual weakness, having within you something higher which can hold out against circumstances.

Such occasions make you enter, first, into contact with that. Afterwards by a methodical discipline you can make the contact continuous; but usually this takes time. But first you get it like that, suddenly, for one reason or another.

(*Long silence*)

This may come with a very strong emotion, with a very great sorrow, a very great enthusiasm. When one is called to perform a fairly exceptional action, in circumstances which are a little exceptional, all of a sudden, one feels something as though breaking or opening within him, and one feels as though he were dominating himself, as though he had climbed up a higher rung and from there was looking at his own existence with the habitual senses. Once one has experienced this, one does not forget; even if only once it has happened, one does not forget it. And one can by concentration reproduce the state at will, later. This is the first step to cultivate it.

Afterwards one can very easily call up this state each time a decision is to be taken, and then one takes it in full awareness of the implications and foreseeing everything that's going to happen. I don't think there's one individual in the world who hasn't experienced it – in any case one cultured individual – at least once in his life, something that breaks and opens... and one understands.

THE MOTHER

I believe more in the power of the atmosphere and of example than of a rigorous teaching. I count more on something awakening in the being through contagion rather than by a methodical, disciplined effort.

Perhaps, after all, something is being prepared and one day it will spring up to the surface.

That is what I hope for.

One day you will tell yourself, "Just think! I have been here so long, I could have learnt so much, realised so much and I never even thought of it!" And then, on that day... well, on that day, just imagine, you are going to wake up all of a sudden to something you never noticed but which is deep within you and *thirsts* for the truth, thirsts for transformation and is ready to make the effort required to realise it. On that day you will go very fast, you will advance with giant strides.... Perhaps you will suddenly feel an *irresistible* need not to live in unconsciousness, in ignorance, in that state in which you do things without knowing why, feel things without understanding why, have contradictory wills, understand nothing about anything, live only by habit, routine, reactions – you take life easy. And one day you are no longer satisfied with that.

It depends, for each one it is different. Most often it is the need to know, to understand; for some it is the need to do what must be done as it should be done; for others it is a vague feeling that behind this life, so unconscious, so futile, so empty of meaning, there is something to find which is *worth* being lived – that there is a reality, a truth behind these falsehoods and illusions.

The starting-point: to want it, truly want it, to need it. The next step: to think, *above all*, of that. A day comes, very quickly, when one is unable to think of anything else.

That is the one thing which counts.

And then... well, one will see what happens.

Something will happen. Surely something will happen. For each one it will take a different form.

THE MOTHER

Mother, how to change one's consciousness?

Naturally, there are many ways, but each person must do it by the means accessible to him; and the indication of the way usually comes spontaneously, through something like an unexpected experience. And for each one, it appears a little differently.

For instance, one may have the perception of the ordinary consciousness which is extended on the surface, horizontally, and works on a plane which is simultaneously the surface of things and has a contact with the superficial outer side of things, people, circumstances; and then, suddenly, for some reason or other – as I say for each one it is different – there is a shifting upwards, and instead of seeing things horizontally, of being at the same level as they are, you suddenly dominate them and see them from above, in their totality, instead of seeing a small number of things immediately next to yourself; it is as though something were drawing you above and making you see as from a mountain-top or an aeroplane. And instead of seeing each detail and seeing it on its own level, you see the whole as one unity, and from far above.

There are many ways of having this experience, but it usually comes to you as if by chance, one fine day.

Or else, one may have an experience which is almost its very opposite but which comes to the same thing. Suddenly one plunges into a depth, one moves away from the thing one perceived, it seems distant, superficial, unimportant; one enters an inner silence or an inner calm or an inward vision of things, a profound feeling, a more intimate perception of circumstances and things, in which all values change. And one becomes aware of a sort of unity, a deep identity which is one in spite of the diverse appearances.

Or else, suddenly also, the sense of limitation disappears and one enters the perception of a kind of indefinite duration beginningless and endless, of something which has always been and always will be.

These experiences come to you suddenly in a flash, for a second, a moment in your life, you don't know why or how.... There are other ways, other experiences – they are innumerable, they vary according to people; but with this, with one minute, one second of such an existence, one catches the tail of the thing. So one must remember that, try to relive it, go to the depths of the experience, recall it, aspire, concentrate. This is the starting point, the end of the guiding thread, the clue. For all those who are destined to find their inner being, the truth of their being, there is always at least one moment in life when they were no longer the same, perhaps just like a lightning-flash – but that is enough. It indicates the road one should take, it is the door that opens on this path. And so you must pass through the door, and with perseverance and an unfailing steadfastness seek to renew the state which will lead you to something more real and more total.

Many ways have always been given, but a way you have been taught, a way you have read about in books or heard from a teacher, does not have the effective value of a spontaneous experience which has come without any apparent reason, and which is simply the blossoming of the soul's awakening, one second of contact with your psychic being which shows you the best way for you, the one most within your reach, which you will then have to follow with perseverance to reach the goal – one second which shows you how to start, the beginning.... Some have this in dreams at night; some have it at any odd time: something one sees which awakens in one this new consciousness, something one hears, a beautiful landscape, beautiful music, or else simply a few words one reads, or else the intensity of concentration in some effort – anything at all, there are a thousand reasons and thousands of ways of having it. But, I repeat, all those who are destined to realise have had this at least once in their life. It may be very fleeting, it may have come when they were very young, but always at least once in one's life one has the experience of what true consciousness is. Well, that is the best indication of the path to be followed.

One may seek within oneself, one may remember, may observe; one must notice what is going on, one must pay attention, that's all. Sometimes, when one sees a generous act, hears of something exceptional, when one witnesses heroism or generosity or greatness of soul, meets someone who shows a special talent or acts in an exceptional and beautiful way, there is a kind of enthusiasm or admiration or gratitude which suddenly awakens in the being and opens the door to a state, a new state of consciousness, a light, a warmth, a joy one did not know before. That too is a way of catching the guiding thread. There are a thousand ways, one has only to be awake and to watch.

First of all, you must feel the necessity for this change of consciousness, accept the idea that it is this, the path which must lead to the goal; and once you admit the principle, you must be watchful. And you will find, you do find it. And once you have found it, you must start walking without any hesitation.

Indeed, the starting-point is to observe oneself, not to

live in a perpetual nonchalance, a perpetual apathy; one must be attentive.

THE MOTHER

One suddenly feels that everything one does, everything one sees, has no meaning, no purpose, but that *there is* something which has a meaning; that essentially one is here on earth for something, that all this – all these movements, all this agitation, all is wastage of force and energy – all that must have a purpose, an aim, and that this uneasiness one feels within oneself, this lack of satisfaction, this need, this *thirst* for something must lead us somewhere else.

And one day, you ask yourself, "But then, why is one born? Why does one die? Why does one suffer? Why does one act?"

You no longer live like a little machine, hardly half-conscious. You want to feel truly, to act truly, to know truly. Then, in ordinary life one searches for books, for people who know a little more than oneself, one begins to seek somebody who can solve these questions, lift the veil of ignorance.

THE MOTHER

When can one say that one has truly entered the spiritual path?

The first sign (it is not the same for everybody) but in a chronological order, I believe, is that everything else appears to you absolutely without importance. Your entire life, all your activities, all your movements continue, if circumstances so arrange things, but they all seem to you utterly unimportant, this is no longer the meaning of your existence. I believe this is the first sign.

There may be another; for example, the feeling that everything is different, of living differently, of a light in the mind which was not there before, of a peace in the heart which was not there before. That does make a change; but the positive change usually comes later, very rarely does it come at first except in a flash at the time of conversion when one has decided to take up the spiritual life. Sometimes, it begins like a great illumination, a deep joy enters into you; but generally, afterwards this goes into the background, for there are too many imperfections still persisting in you.... It is not disgust, it is not contempt, but everything appears to you so uninteresting that it is truly not worth the trouble of attending to it. For instance, when you are in the midst of certain physical conditions, pleasant or unpleasant (the two extremes meet), you say to yourself, "It was so important to me, all that? But it has no importance at all!" You have the impression that you have truly turned over to the other side.

THE MOTHER

As long as the mind is convinced that it is the summit of human consciousness, that there is nothing beyond and above it, it takes its own functioning to be a perfect one and is fully satisfied with the progress it can make within the limits of this functioning, and with an increase of clarity, precision, complexity, suppleness, plasticity in its movements.

It always has a spontaneous tendency to feel very satisfied with itself and with what it can do, and if there were no greater force than its own, a higher power which irrefutably shows it its own limitations, its poverty, it would never make any effort to find its way out of all that by the right door: liberation into a higher and truer mode of being.

When the spiritual force is able to act, when it begins to have an influence, it jolts the mind's self-satisfaction and, by continuous pressure, begins to make it feel that beyond it there is something higher and truer; then a little of its characteristic vanity gives way under this influence and as soon as it realises that it is limited, ignorant, incapable of reaching the true truth, liberation begins with the possibility of opening to something beyond. But it must *feel* the power, the beauty, the force of this beyond to be able to surrender. It must be able to perceive its incapacity and its limitations in the presence of something higher than itself, otherwise how could it ever feel its own weakness!

Sometimes one single contact is enough, something that makes a little rent in that self-satisfaction; then the yearning to go beyond, the need for a purer light awaken, and with this awakening comes the aspiration to win them, and with the aspiration liberation begins, and one day, breaking all limits, one blossoms in the infinite Light.

If there were not this constant Pressure, simultaneously from within and without, from above and from the profoundest depths, nothing would ever change.

Even with that, how much time is required for things to change! What obstinate resistance in this lower nature, what blind and stupid attachment to the animal ways of the being, what a refusal to liberate oneself!...

When you open to the Spirit within you it brings you a first foretaste of that higher life which alone is worth living, then comes the will to rise to that, the hope of reaching it, the certitude that this is possible, and finally the strength to make the necessary effort and the resolution to go to the very end.

First one must wake up, then one can conquer.

THE MOTHER

III

GROWTH OF CONSCIOUSNESS
BASIC REQUISITES

Yoga-Siddhi, the perfection that comes from the practice of Yoga, can be best attained by the combined working of four great instruments. There is, first, the knowledge of the truths, principles, powers and processes that govern the realisation – *śāstra*. Next comes a patient and persistent action on the lines laid down by the knowledge, the force of our personal effort – *utsāha*. There intervenes, third, uplifting our knowledge and effort into the domain of spiritual experience, the direct suggestion, example and influence of the Teacher – *guru*. Last comes the instrumentality of Time – *kāla*; for in all things there is a cycle of their action and a period of the divine movement.

SRI AUROBINDO

Until we know the Truth (not mentally but by experience, by change of consciousness) we need the soul's faith to sustain us and hold on to the Truth – but when we live in the knowledge, this faith is changed into knowledge.

SRI AUROBINDO

There is one indispensable condition, sincerity.

SRI AUROBINDO

Sincerity is the safeguard, the protection, the guide, and finally the transforming power.

THE MOTHER

GROWTH OF CONSCIOUSNESS
BASIC REQUISITES

Aspiration

The development of the experience in its rapidity, its amplitude, the intensity and power of its result, depends primarily, in the beginning of the path and long after, on the aspiration and personal effort of the Sadhaka. The process of Yoga is a turning of the human soul from the egoistic state of consciousness absorbed in the outward appearances and attractions of things to a higher state in which the Transcendent and Universal can pour itself into the individual mould and transform it. The first determining element of the Siddhi is, therefore, the intensity of the turning, the force which directs the soul inward. The power of aspiration of the heart, the force of the will, the concentration of the mind, the perseverance and determination of the applied energy are the measure of that intensity. The ideal Sadhaka should be able to say in the Biblical phrase, "My zeal for the Lord has eaten me up." It is this zeal for the Lord, *utsāha*, the zeal of the whole nature for its divine results, *vyākulatā*, the heart's eagerness for the attainment of the Divine, – that devours the ego and breaks up the limitations of its petty and narrow mould for the full and wide reception of that which it seeks, that which, being universal, exceeds and, being transcendent, surpasses even the largest and highest individual self and nature.

SRI AUROBINDO

"*A psychic fire within must be lit....*" SRI AUROBINDO

Isn't the psychic fire always lit?

It is not always lit.

Then how to light it?

By aspiration.

By the will for progress, by the urge towards perfection.

Above all, it is the will for progress and self-purification which lights the fire. The will for progress. Those who have a strong will, when they turn it towards spiritual progress and purification, automatically light the fire within themselves.

And each defect one wants to cure or each progress one wants to make – if all that is thrown into the fire, it burns with a new intensity. And this is not an image, it is a fact in the subtle physical. One can feel the warmth of the flame, one can see in the subtle physical the light of the flame. And when there is something in the nature which prevents one from advancing and one throws it into this fire, it begins to burn and the flame becomes more intense.

THE MOTHER

"*This is the first thing necessary – aspiration for the Divine.*"

THE MOTHER
(Questions and Answers 1929, 7 April)

The first movement of aspiration is this: you have a kind

of vague sensation that behind the universe there is something which is worth knowing, which is probably (for you do not yet know it) the only thing worth living for, which can connect you with the Truth; something on which the universe depends but which does not depend upon the universe, something which still escapes your comprehension but which seems to you to be behind all things.... I have said here much more than the majority of people feel about the thing, but this is the beginning of the first aspiration – to know that, not to live in this perpetual falsehood where things are so perverted and artificial, this would be something pleasant; to find something that is worth living for.

> *"The next thing you have to do is to tend this aspiration, to keep it always alert and awake and living."*
>
> *Ibid.*

Instead of telling yourself once in a while, "Oh, yes! I am thinking of finding the Divine", just when there is something unpleasant, when you are a little disgusted because you feel tired – indeed, there are very many flimsy reasons – all of a sudden you remember that there is such a thing as yoga, something like the Divine to know who can get you out of this flatness of life.

> *"And for that what is required is concentration – concentration upon the Divine with a view to an integral and absolute consecration to its Will and Purpose."*
>
> *Ibid.*

This is the second step. That is to say, you begin wanting

to find and know the Divine and live it. You must feel at
the same time that the thing is so precious, so important
that your entire life is not sufficient for acquiring it. Then,
the first movement is a self-giving; you tell yourself, "I do
not want any longer to belong to myself, for the sake of
my little personal satisfaction, I wish to belong to this
marvellous thing which one must find, must know, must
live and for which I aspire."

THE MOTHER

What is the difference between prayer and aspiration?

Prayer is a much more external thing, generally about a
precise fact, and always formulated for it is the formula
that makes the prayer. One may have an aspiration and
transcribe it as a prayer, but aspiration goes beyond
prayer in every way. It is much closer and much more, as
it were, self-forgetful, living only in the thing one wants to
be or do, and the offering of all that one wants to do to the
Divine....

To be clearer, we may say that prayer is always formulated in words; but the words may have different values
according to the state in which they are formulated.
Prayer is a formulated thing and one may aspire. But it is
difficult to pray without praying to someone. For instance,
those who have a conception of the universe from which
they have more or less driven out the idea of the Divine
(there are many people of this kind; this idea troubles
them – the idea that there is someone who knows all, can
do everything and who is so formidably greater than they
that there can be no comparison; that's a bit troublesome

for their *amour-propre*; so they try to make a world without the Divine), these people evidently cannot pray, for to whom would they pray? Unless they pray to themselves, which is not the custom! But one can aspire for something without having any faith in the Divine. There are people who do not believe in the existence of a God, but who have faith in progress. They have the idea that the world is in constant progress and that this progress will go on indefinitely without stopping, towards an ever greater betterment. Well, these people can have a very great aspiration for progress, and they don't even need any idea of a divine existence for that. Aspiration necessarily implies a faith but not necessarily faith in a divine being; whilst prayer cannot exist if it is not addressed to a divine being. And pray to what? One does not pray to something that has no personality! One prays to someone who can hear us. If there is nobody to hear us, how could one pray? Hence, if one prays, this means that, even when one doesn't acknowledge it, one has faith in somebody infinitely higher than us, infinitely more powerful, who can change our destiny and change us also, if one prays so as to be heard. That is the essential difference.

So the more intellectual people admit aspiration and say that prayer is something inferior. The mystics tell you that aspiration is all very well but if you want to be really heard and want the Divine to listen to you, you must pray, and pray with the simplicity of a child, a perfect candour, that is, a perfect trust: "I need this or that (whether it be a moral need or a physical or material need), well, I ask You for it, give it to me."... To aspire it is not necessary to direct the aspiration to someone, towards someone. One has an aspiration for a certain state of being, for knowledge, for a realisation, a state of consciousness; one aspires for something, but it is not necessarily a prayer; prayer is something additional.

THE MOTHER

Sincerity

What is the fundamental virtue to be cultivated in order to prepare for the spiritual life?

I have said this many times, but this is an opportunity to repeat it: it is *sincerity*.

A sincerity which must become total and absolute, for sincerity *alone* is your protection on the spiritual path. If you are not sincere, at the very next step you are sure to fall and break your head. All kinds of forces, wills, influences, entities are there, on the look-out for the least little rift in this sincerity and they immediately rush in through that rift and begin to throw you into confusion.

Therefore, before doing anything, beginning anything, trying anything, be sure *first of all* that you are not only as sincere as you can be, but have the intention of becoming still more so.

For that is your only protection.

THE MOTHER

Sincere is simply an adjective meaning that the will must be a true will. If you simply think "I aspire" and do things inconsistent with the aspiration, or follow your desires or open yourself to contrary influences, then it is not a sincere will.

SRI AUROBINDO

Men are always mixed and there are qualities and defects mingled together almost inextricably in their nature. What a man wants to be or wants others to see in him or what he is sometimes on one side of his nature or in some relations can be very different from what he is in the actual fact or in other relations or on another side of his nature. To be absolutely sincere, straightforward, open, is not an easy achievement for human nature. It is only by spiritual endeavour that one can realise it – and to do it needs a severity of introspective self-vision, an unsparing scrutiny of self-observation of which many sadhaks and yogis even are not capable....

SRI AUROBINDO

What does "sincerity" mean, exactly?

There are several degrees of sincerity.

The most elementary degree is not to say one thing and think another, claim one thing and want another. For example, what happens quite often: to say, "I want to make progress, and I want to get rid of my defects" and, at the same time, to cherish one's defects in the con-sciousness and take great care to hide them so that nobody intervenes and sends them off. This indeed is a very common phenomenon. This is already the second degree. The first degree, you see, is when someone claims, for example, to have a very great aspiration and to want the spiritual life and, at the same time, does completely... how to put it?... shamelessly, things which are most contradictory to the spiritual life. This is indeed a degree of sincerity, rather of insincerity, which is most obvious.

But there is a second degree which I have just described to you, which is like this: there is one part of the being which has an aspiration and says, even thinks, even feels that it would very much like to get rid of defects, imperfections; and then, at the same time, other parts which hide these defects and imperfections very carefully so as not to be compelled to expose them and get over them. This is very common.

And finally, if we go far enough, if we push the description far enough, so long as there is a part of the being which contradicts the central aspiration for the Divine, one is not perfectly sincere. That is to say, a perfect sincerity is something extremely rare. And most commonly, very very frequently, when there are things in one's nature which one does not like, one takes the greatest care to hide them from oneself, one finds favourable explanations or simply makes a little movement, like this (*gesture*). You have noticed that when things move like this you can't see them clearly. Well, where the defect is seated, there is a kind of vibration which does this, and so your sight is not clear, you no longer see your defects. And this is automatic. Well, all these are insincerities.

And perfect sincerity comes when at the centre of the being there is the consciousness of the divine Presence, the consciousness of the divine Will, and when the entire being, like a luminous, clear, transparent whole, expresses this in all its details. This indeed is true sincerity.

When, at any moment, whatever may happen, the being has given itself to the Divine and wants only the divine Will, when, no matter what is going on in the being, at any moment whatever, always, the whole being in perfect unanimity can say to the Divine and feels for the

Divine, "Let Thy Will be done", when it is spontaneous, total, integral, *then* you are sincere. But until this is established, it is a mixed sincerity, more or less mixed, right up to the point where one is not at all sincere.

THE MOTHER

One must never pretend that one *is*: one must *be*, spontaneously.
    This is sincerity.

THE MOTHER

Faith

Faith does not depend upon experience; it is something that is there before experience. When one starts the yoga, it is not usually on the strength of experience, but on the strength of faith. It is so not only in yoga and the spiritual life, but in ordinary life also. All men of action, discoverers, inventors, creators of knowledge proceed by faith and, until the proof is made or the thing done, they go on in spite of disappointment, failure, disproof, denial because of something in them that tells them that this is the truth, the thing that must be followed and done. Ramakrishna even went so far as to say, when asked whether blind faith was not wrong, that blind faith was the only kind to have, for faith is either blind or it is not faith but something else – reasoned inference, proved conviction or ascertained knowledge.

Faith is the soul's witness to something not yet manifested, achieved or realised, but which yet the Knower within us, even in the absence of all indications, feels to be true or supremely worth following or achieving. This thing within us can last even when there is no fixed belief in the mind, even when the vital struggles and revolts and refuses. Who is there that practises the yoga and has not his periods, long periods of disappointment and failure and disbelief and darkness? But there is something that sustains him and even goes on in spite of himself, because it feels that what it followed after was yet true and it more than feels, it knows. The fundamental faith in yoga is this, inherent in the soul, that the Divine exists and the Divine is the one thing to be followed after – nothing else in life is worth having in comparison with that. So long as a man has that faith, he is marked for the spiritual life and I will say that, even if his nature is full of obstacles and crammed with denials and difficulties, and even if he has many years of struggle, he is marked out for success in the spiritual life.

                                        SRI AUROBINDO

… faith in the spiritual sense is not a mental belief which can waver and change. It can wear that form in the mind, but that belief is not the faith itself, it is only its external form. Just as the body, the external form, can change but the spirit remains the same, so it is here. Faith is a certitude in the soul which does not depend on reasoning, on this or that mental idea, on circumstances, on this or that passing condition of the mind or the vital or the body. It may be hidden, eclipsed, may even seem to be quenched, but it reappears again after the storm or the eclipse; it is seen burning still in the soul when one has thought that it was extinguished for ever. The mind may be a shifting sea of doubts and yet that faith may be there within and, if so, it will keep even the doubt-racked mind in the way so that it goes on in spite of itself towards its destined goal. Faith is a spiritual certitude of the spiritual, the divine, the soul's ideal, something that clings to that even when it is not fulfilled in life, even when the immediate facts or the persistent circumstances seem to deny it. This is a common experience in the life of the human being; if it were not so, man would be the plaything of a changing mind or a sport of circumstances.

SRI AUROBINDO

"Just as the strong wind has no hold upon a mighty rock, so Mara has no hold upon a man... who is endowed with unshakable faith and who wastes not his energies." — The Dhammapada

What the Dhammapada means when it speaks of faith is not at all the belief in a dogma or a religion, it is not even faith in the teaching of the Master; it is faith in one's own possibilities, the certitude that whatever the difficulties, whatever the obstacles, whatever the imperfections, even the negations in the being, one is born for the realisation and one *will* realise.

The will must never falter, the effort must be persevering and the faith unshakable. Then instead of spending years to realise what one has to realise, one can do it in a few months, sometimes even in a few days and, if there is sufficient intensity, in a few hours. That is to say, you can take a position within yourself and no bad will that attacks the realisation will have any more power over you than the storm has over a rock.

After that, the way is no longer difficult; it becomes extraordinarily interesting.

THE MOTHER

"To be always observing faults and wrong movements brings depression and discourages the faith" (Sri Aurobindo). *How does it discourage the faith?*

The faith spoken about is faith in the divine Grace and the final success of the undertaking. You have begun the yoga and have faith that you will go through to the end of your yoga. But if you spend your time looking at all that prevents you from advancing, then finally you say, "Ah, I shall never succeed! It is not possible. If it goes on in this way, I shall never get there." So this is to lose one's faith. One must always keep the faith that one is sure to succeed.

Many people begin, and then after some time come and tell you, "Oh, I shall never be able to go through. I have too many difficulties." So this means not having faith. If one has started, one begins with the faith that one will reach the goal. Well, this faith should be kept till the very end. Keeping one's faith, one attains the end. But if in the middle of the road you turn back saying, "No, I can't", then, obviously you will not reach the end. Some people start on the way and then, after some time, they find it heavy-going, tiring, difficult, and also that they themselves, their legs, don't walk well, their feet begin to ache, etc. You see, they say, "Oh, it is very hard to go

forward." So instead of saying, "I have started, I shall go
through", which is the only thing to do, they stand there,
stop there, lamenting and saying, "Oh, I shall never be
able to succeed", and then they leave the path. So,
obviously, if they leave the path, they will never succeed.
This is to lose one's faith.

To keep one's faith is to say, "Good, I have difficulties
but I am going on." Despair — that's what cuts off your
legs, stops you, leaves you like this: "It is over, I can't go
on any longer." It is indeed finished, and that's something
which should not be allowed.

THE MOTHER.

One must watch over one's faith as one watches over the
birth of something *infinitely* precious, and protect it very
carefully from everything that can impair it.

In the ignorance and darkness of the beginning, faith is
the most direct expression of the Divine Power which
comes to fight and conquer.

THE MOTHER

The Teaching – Mental Preparation

Nothing can be taught to the mind which is not already
concealed as potential knowledge in the unfolding soul of
the creature. So also all perfection of which the outer man
is capable, is only a realising of the eternal perfection of
the Spirit within him. We know the Divine and become
the Divine, because we are That already in our secret
nature. All teaching is a revealing, all becoming is an

unfolding. Self-attainment is the secret; self-knowledge and an increasing consciousness are the means and the process.

The usual agency of this revealing is the Word, the thing heard (*śruta*). The Word may come to us from within; it may come to us from without. But in either case, it is only an agency for setting the hidden knowledge to work. The word within may be the utterance of the inmost soul in us which is always open to the Divine or it may be the word of the secret and universal Teacher who is seated in the hearts of all. There are rare cases in which none other is needed, for all the rest of the Yoga is an unfolding under that constant touch and guidance; the lotus of the knowledge discloses itself from within by the power of irradiating effulgence which proceeds from the Dweller in the lotus of the heart. Great indeed, but few are those to whom self-knowledge from within is thus sufficient and who do not need to pass under the dominant influence of a written book or a living teacher.

Ordinarily, the Word from without, representative of the Divine, is needed as an aid in the work of self-unfolding; and it may be either a word from the past or the more powerful word of the living Guru. In some cases this representative word is only taken as a sort of excuse for the inner power to awaken and manifest; it is, as it were, a concession of the omnipotent and omniscient Divine to the generality of a law that governs Nature. Thus it is said in the Upanishads of Krishna, son of Devaki, that he received a word of the Rishi Ghora and had the knowledge. So Ramakrishna, having attained by his own internal effort the central illumination, accepted several teachers in the different paths of Yoga, but always showed in the manner and swiftness of his realisation that this acceptance was a concession to the general rule by which effective knowledge must be received as by a disciple from a Guru.

But usually the representative influence occupies a much larger place in the life of the Sadhaka. If the Yoga is guided by a received written Shastra, – some Word from the past which embodies the experience of former Yogins, – it may be practised either by personal effort alone or with the aid of a Guru. The spiritual knowledge is then gained through meditation on the truths that are taught and it is made living and conscious by their realisation in the personal experience; the Yoga proceeds by the results of prescribed methods taught in a Scripture or a tradition and reinforced and illumined by the instructions of the Master. This is a narrower practice, but safe and effective within its limits, because it follows a well-beaten track to a long familiar goal.

For the Sadhaka of the integral Yoga it is necessary to remember that no written Shastra, however great its authority or however large its spirit, can be more than a partial expression of the eternal Knowledge. He will use, but never bind himself even by the greatest Scripture. Where the Scripture is profound, wide, catholic, it may exercise upon him an influence for the highest good and of incalculable importance. It may be associated in his experience with his awakening to crowning verities and his realisation of the highest experiences. His Yoga may be governed for a long time by one Scripture or by several succesively, – if it is in the line of the great Hindu tradition, by the Gita, for example, the Upanishads, the Veda. Or it may be a good part of his development to include in its material a richly varied experience of the truths of many Scriptures and make the future opulent with all that is best in the past. But in the end he must take his station, or better still, if he can, always and from the beginning he must live in his own soul beyond the written Truth, – *śabdabrahmātivartate* – beyond all that he has heard and all that he has yet to hear, – *śrotavyasya śrutasya ca*. For he is not the Sadhaka of a book or of many books; he is a Sadhaka of the Infinite.

Another kind of Shastra is not Scripture, but a statement of the science and methods, the effective principles and way of working of the path of Yoga which the Sadhaka elects to follow. Each path has its Shastra, either written or traditional, passing from mouth to mouth through a long line of Teachers. In India a great authority, a high reverence even is ordinarily attached to the written or traditional teaching. All the lines of the Yoga are supposed to be fixed and the Teacher who has received the Shastra by tradition and realised it in practice guides the disciple along the immemorial tracks. One often even hears the objection urged against a new practice, a new Yogic teaching, the adoption of a new formula, "It is not according to the Shastra." But neither in fact nor in the actual practice of the Yogins is there really any such entire rigidity of an iron door shut against new truth, fresh revelation, widened experience. The written or traditional teaching expresses the knowledge and experiences of many centuries systematised, organised, made attainable to the beginner. Its importance and utility are therefore immense. But a great freedom of variation and development is always practicable. Even so highly scientific a system as Rajayoga can be practised on other lines than the organised method of Patanjali. Each of the three paths, *trimārga*,* breaks into many bypaths which meet again at the goal. The general knowledge on which the Yoga depends is fixed, but the order, the succession, the devices, the forms must be allowed to vary; for the needs and particular impulsions of the individual nature have to be satisfied even while the general truths remain firm and constant.

SRI AUROBINDO

Always the most interesting cases for me have been those of people who had read nothing but had a very ardent aspiration and came to me saying, "Something funny has happened to me, I had this extraordinary experience, what can it mean truly?" And then they describe a movement, a vibration, a force, a light, whatever it might be, it depends on each one, and they describe this, that it happened like that and came like that, and then this happened and then that, and what does it all mean, all this? Then here one is on the right side. One knows that it is not an imagined experience, that it is a sincere, spontaneous one, and this always has a power of transformation much greater than the experience that was brought about by a mental knowledge.

Then, Mother, this means that it is better not to read?

On condition that one truly has within himself the ardour of aspiration. If you are born for this, for the yoga, and this is the thing which dominates all your existence, that

* The triple path of Knowledge, Devotion and Works.

you feel, yes, before knowing anything, that you need to find something which is in you, then sometimes a word is enough, a conversation which simply orients you – it is enough. But for those who are seeking, who grope, who are not absolutely sure, who are pulled this way and that, have many interests in life, are not steady, stabilised in their will for realisation, it is very good to read, because it puts them in touch with the subject, it gives them some interest in the thing.

What I mean is that every definite mental formation always gives a particular colouring to the experience. As for example, with all people brought up in a certain religion their experiences will always be coloured by this religion; and in fact, to reach the very source of the thing one must free oneself from the external formation.

But there is a kind of reading which awakens in you an interest in the thing and can help you in the first seekings. Usually, even if one has had experiences one needs a contact of thought or idea with the thing so that the effort may be crystallized more consciously. But the more one knows, the more one must be absolutely sincere in his experience, that is, he must not use the formative power of his mind to imagine and so create the experience in himself. From the point of view of orientation it can be useful: but from the point of view of the experience, it takes away from it its dynamic value, it has not the intensity of an experience which comes because the moral and spiritual conditions necessary for it to occur have been fulfilled. There is the whole mental conditioning which is added and which takes away something of the spontaneity. All this is a matter of proportion. Each one must find the exact amount he needs, how much of reading, how much meditation, how much concentration, how much... It is different for each one.

THE MOTHER

"At present your experiences are on the mental plane...." Sri Aurobindo

What does "on the mental plane" mean?

Well, these are experiences concerning thought, mental activity, the understanding of things, the observation of things, thought, deduction, reasoning, the contact with teaching, knowledge, the result of this knowledge on your understanding – all these things which are purely mental. And in fact one should always begin with that.

If one has vital experiences – for example, visions – certain vital experiences without having a sufficient mental preparation, this may result in destroying one's balance and, in any case, one understands nothing of what is happening and it is practically useless, if not harmful. On the other hand, if to begin with, one has developed his understanding, has studied, has understood and knows the reasons for things, and the goal of yoga, for instance, and if one has studied the methods of attaining it – indeed, the whole mental approach to the subject – then, when an experience comes one has a chance of being able to understand what it is; otherwise one understands nothing. A sufficient mental preparation is needed – if not a complete one at least a sufficient one – to be able to understand a little the experiences which come.

THE MOTHER

The Teacher

The spiritual progress of most human beings demands an extraneous support, an object of faith outside us. It needs an external image of God; or it needs a human representative, – Incarnation, Prophet or Guru; or it demands both and receives them. For according to the need of the human soul the Divine manifests himself as deity, as human divine or in simple humanity, – using that thick disguise, which so successfully conceals the Godhead, for a means of transmission of his guidance.

The Hindu discipline of spirituality provides for this need of the soul by the conceptions of the Ishta Devata, the Avatar and the Guru. By the Ishta Devata, the chosen deity, is meant, – not some inferior Power, but a name and form of the transcendent and universal Godhead. Almost all religions either have as their base or make use of some such name and form of the Divine. Its necessity for the human soul is evident. God is the All and more than the All. But that which is more than the All, how shall man conceive? And even the All is at first too hard for him; for he himself in his active consciousness is a limited and selective formation and can open himself only to that which is in harmony with his limited nature. There are things in the All which are too hard for his comprehension or seem too terrible to his sensitive emotions and cowering sensations. Or, simply, he cannot conceive as the Divine, cannot approach or cannot recognise something that is too much out of the circle of his ignorant or partial conceptions. It is necessary for him to conceive God in his own image or in some form that is beyond himself but consonant with his highest tendencies and seizable by his feelings or his intelligence. Otherwise it would be difficult for him to come into contact and communion with the Divine.

Even then his nature calls for a human intermediary so that he may feel the Divine in something entirely close to his own humanity and sensible in a human influence and example. This call is satisfied by the Divine manifest in a human appearance, the Incarnation, the Avatar – Krishna, Christ, Buddha. Or if this is too hard for him to conceive, the Divine represents himself through a less marvellous intermediary, – Prophet or Teacher. For many who cannot conceive or are unwilling to accept the Divine Man, are ready to open themselves to the supreme man, terming him not incarnation but world-teacher or divine representative.

This also is not enough; a living influence, a living example, a present instruction is needed. For it is only the few who can make the past Teacher and his teaching, the past Incarnation and his example and influence a living force in their lives. For this need also the Hindu discipline provides in the relation of the Guru and the disciple. The Guru may sometimes be the Incarnation or World-Teacher; but it is sufficient that he should represent to the disciple the divine wisdom, convey to him something of the divine ideal or make him feel the realised relation of the human soul with the Eternal....

... It is not sufficient to worship Krishna, Christ or Buddha without, if there is not the revealing and the formation of the Buddha, the Christ or Krishna in ourselves. And all other aids equally have no other purpose; each is a bridge between man's unconverted state and the revelation of the Divine within him.

SRI AUROBINDO

Teaching, example, influence, – these are the three instruments of the Guru. But the wise Teacher will not seek to impose himself or his opinions on the passive acceptance of the receptive mind; he will throw in only what is productive and sure as a seed which will grow under the divine fostering within. He will seek to awaken much more than to instruct; he will aim at the growth of the faculties and the experiences by a natural process and free expansion. He will give a method as an aid, as a utilisable device, not as an imperative formula or a fixed routine. And he will be on his guard against any turning of the means into a limitation, against the mechanising of process. His whole business is to awaken the divine light and set working the divine force of which he himself is only a means and an aid, a body or a channel.

The example is more powerful than the instruction; but it is not the example of the outward acts nor that of the personal character, which is of most importance. These have their place and their utility; but what will most stimulate aspiration in others is the central fact of the divine realisation within him governing his whole life and inner state and all his activities. This is the universal and essential element; the rest belongs to individual person and circumstance. It is the dynamic realisation that the Sadhaka must feel and reproduce in himself according to his own nature; he need not strive after an imitation from outside which may well be sterilising rather than productive of right and natural fruits.

Influence is more important than example. Influence is not the outward authority of the Teacher over his disciple, but the power of his contact, of his presence, of the nearness of his soul to the soul of another, infusing into it, even though in silence, that which he himself is and possesses. This is the supreme sign of the Master. For the greatest Master is much less a Teacher than a Presence pouring the divine consciousness and its constituting light and power and purity and bliss into all who are receptive around him.

And it shall also be a sign of the teacher of the integral Yoga that he does not arrogate to himself Guruhood in a humanly vain and self-exalting spirit. His work, if he has one, is a trust from above, he himself a channel, a vessel or a representative. He is a man helping his brothers, a child leading children, a Light kindling other lights, an awakened Soul awakening souls, at highest a Power or Presence of the Divine calling to him other powers of the Divine.

SRI AUROBINDO

The Western mind always finds it difficult to submit totally to a Guru and without total and unquestioning surrender to the Guru his help to you is paralysed. That is why generally I advise westerners to find the guidance and the Presence within themselves; it is true that this process is very often open to uncertainty and self-deception, mistaking some voice of the ego in disguise for the Divine's guidance.

In both cases, it is only an absolute sincerity and an unmixed humility that can be your safeguard.

THE MOTHER

If you have faith and confidence, it is not the human form

of the guru that you worship, but the Supreme Lord who manifests through him.

... Give yourself unreservedly to the Supreme Lord through whatever channel helps you.

THE MOTHER

The Guru is the channel or the representative or the manifestation of the Divine, according to the measure of his personality or his attainment; but whatever he is, it is to the Divine that one opens in opening to him; and if something is determined by the power of the channel, more is determined by the inherent and intrinsic attitude of the receiving consciousness, an element that comes out in the surface mind as simple trust or direct unconditional self-giving, and once that is there, the essential things can be gained even from one who seems to others than the disciple an inferior spiritual source, and the rest will grow up in the sadhak of itself by the Grace of the Divine, even if the human being in the Guru cannot give it.

SRI AUROBINDO

Patience and Right Attitude

It is certain that an ardent aspiration for the Divine helps one to progress, but patience is also needed. For it is a very big change that has to be made and, although there can be moments of great rapidity, it is never all the time like that. Old things try to stick as much as possible; the new that come have to develop and the consciousness takes time to assimilate them and make them normal to the nature.

SRI AUROBINDO

The sadhana is a difficult one and time should not be grudged; it is only in the last stages that a very great and constant rapidity of progress can be confidently expected.

SRI AUROBINDO

Determination is needed and a firm patience, not to be discouraged by this or that failure. It is a change in the habit of the physical nature and that needs a long patient work of detail.

SRI AUROBINDO

Impatience is always a mistake, it does not help but hinders. A quiet happy faith and confidence is the best foundation for sadhana; for the rest a constant opening wide of oneself to receive with an aspiration which may be intense, but must always be calm and steady. Full yogic realisation does not come all at once, it comes after a long preparation of the Adhar which may take a long time.

SRI AUROBINDO

The power needed in yoga is the power to go through effort, difficulty or trouble without getting fatigued, depressed, discouraged or impatient and without breaking off the effort or giving up one's aim or resolution.

SRI AUROBINDO

Whatever method is used, persistence and perseverance are essential. For whatever method is used, the complexity of the natural resistance will be there to combat it.

SRI AUROBINDO

The inner spiritual progress does not depend on outer conditions so much as in the way we react to them from within – that has always been the ultimate verdict of spiritual experience. It is why we insist on taking the right attitude and persisting in it, on an inner state not dependent on outer circumstances, a state of equality and calm, if it cannot be at once of inner happiness, on going more and more within and looking from within outwards instead of living in the surface mind which is always at the mercy of the shocks and blows of life. It is only from that inner state that one can be stronger than life and its disturbing forces and hope to conquer.

To remain quiet within, firm in the will to go through, refusing to be disturbed or discouraged by difficulties or fluctuations, that is one of the first things to be learned in the Path. To do otherwise is to encourage the instability of consciousness, the difficulty of keeping experience of which you complain. It is only if you keep quiet and steady within that the lines of experience can go on with some steadiness – though they are never without periods of interruption and fluctuation; but these, if properly treated, can then become periods of assimilation and exhaustion of difficulty rather than denials of sadhana.

A spiritual atmosphere is more important than outer conditions; if one can get that and also create one's own spiritual air to breathe in and live in it, that is the true condition of progress.

SRI AUROBINDO

When we make an effort to do better but don't see any progress, we feel discouraged. What is the best thing to do?

Not to be discouraged! Despondency leads nowhere.

To begin with, the first thing to tell yourself is that you are almost entirely incapable of knowing whether you are making progress or not, for very often what seems to us to be a state of stagnation is a long – sometimes long, but in any case not endless – preparation for a leap forward. We sometimes seem to be marking time for weeks or months, and then suddenly something that was being prepared makes its appearance, and we see that there is quite a considerable change and *on several points* at a time.

As with everything in yoga, the effort for progress must be made for the love of the effort for progress. The joy of effort, the aspiration for progress must be enough in themselves, quite independent of the result. Everything one does in yoga must be done for the joy of doing it, and not in view of the result one wants to obtain.... Indeed, in life, always, in all things, the result does not belong to us. And if we want to keep the right attitude, we must act, feel, think, strive spontaneously, for *that* is what we must do, and not in view of the result to be obtained.

As soon as we think of the result we begin to bargain and that takes away all sincerity from the effort. You make an effort to progress because you feel within you the need, the *imperative* need to make an effort and progress; and this effort is the gift you offer to the Divine Consciousness in you, the Divine Consciousness in the Universe, it is your way of expressing your gratitude, offering your self; and whether this results in progress or not is of no importance. You will progress when it is decided that the time has come to progress and not because you desire it.

THE MOTHER

To realise anything one must be patient, and the vaster and more important the realisation, the greater the patience must be.

THE MOTHER

...progressive sadhana is enormously helped by an assured faith and confidence. Such a confidence helps to realise, for it is dynamic and tends to fulfil itself.

SRI AUROBINDO

There is nothing spiritually wrong in being glad and cheerful, on the contrary it is the right thing... There is a sunlit path as well as a gloomy one and it is the better of the two....

SRI AUROBINDO

IV

GROWTH OF CONSCIOUSNESS
FIRST STEPS AND FOUNDATION

The Rajayogis are right in putting purification in front of everything – as I was also right in putting it in front along with concentration in *The Synthesis of Yoga*. You have only to look about you to see that experiences and even realisations cannot bring one to the goal if this is not done – at any moment they can fall owing to the vital still being impure and full of ego.

SRI AUROBINDO

Equanimity and peace in all conditions, in all parts of the being is the first foundation of the yogic status.... Peace is the first condition without which nothing else can be stable.

SRI AUROBINDO

GROWTH OF CONSCIOUSNESS
FIRST STEPS AND FOUNDATION

Purification

The first necessity of preparation is the purifying of all the members of our being; especially, for the path of knowledge, the purification of the understanding, the key that shall open the door of Truth; and a purified understanding is hardly possible without the purification of the other members. An unpurified heart, an unpurified sense, an unpurified life confuse the understanding, disturb its data, distort its conclusions, darken its seeing, misapply its knowledge; an unpurified physical system clogs or chokes up its action. There must be an integral purity. Here also there is an interdependence; for the purification of each member of our being profits by the clarifying of every other, the progressive tranquillisation of the emotional heart helping for instance the purification of the understanding while equally a purified understanding imposes calm and light on the turbid and darkened workings of the yet impure emotions. It may even be said that while each member of our being has its own proper principles of purification, yet it is the purified understanding that in man is the most potent cleanser of his turbid and disordered being and most sovereignly imposes their right working on his other members. Knowledge, says the Gita, is the sovereign purity; light is the source of all clearness and harmony even as the darkness of ignorance is the cause of all our stumblings.

SRI AUROBINDO

Do not be over-eager for experiences; for experiences you can always get, having once broken the barrier between the physical mind and the subtle planes. What you have to aspire for most is the improved quality of the recipient consciousness in you, discrimination in the mind, the unattached impersonal Witness look on all that goes on in you and around you, purity in the vital, calm equanimity, enduring patience, absence of pride and the sense of greatness – and more especially, the development of the psychic being in you – surrender, self-giving, psychic humility, devotion. It is a consciousness made up of these things, cast in this mould, that can bear without breaking, stumbling or deviation into error the rush of lights, power and experiences from the supraphysical planes. An entire perfection in these respects is hardly possible until the whole nature from the higher mind to the subconscient physical is made one in the light that is greater than the mind, but a sufficient foundation and a consciousness always self-observant, vigilant and growing in these things is indispensable – for perfect purification is the basis of the perfect Siddhi.

Sri Aurobindo

One is truly perfectly pure only when the whole being, in all its elements and all its movements, adheres fully, exclusively, to the divine Will. This indeed is total purity. It does not depend on any moral or social law, any mental convention of any kind. It depends exclusively on this: when all the elements and all the movements of the being adhere exclusively and totally to the divine Will.

Now, there are stages, there are degrees. For example,

insincerity, which is one of the greatest impurities, always arises from the fact that a movement or a set of movements, an element of the being or a number of elements, want to follow their own will and not be the expression of the divine Will. So this produces in the being either a revolt or a falsehood. I don't mean that one tells lies, but I mean that one is in a state of falsehood, of insincerity. And then, the consequences are more or less serious and more or less extensive according to the gravity of the movement itself and its importance. But these, if one sees from the point of view of purity, these are the real impurities.

For example, if you take your stand on a moral viewpoint – which is itself altogether wrong from the spiritual point of view – there are people who apparently lead an altogether perfectly moral life, who conform to all the social laws, all the customs, the moral conventions, and who are a mass of impurity – from the spiritual point of view these beings are profoundly impure. On the other hand there are some poor people who do things... who are born, for instance, with a sense of freedom, and do things which are not considered very respectable from the social or moral point view, and who can be in a state of inner aspiration and inner sincerity which makes them infinitely purer than the others. This is one of the big difficulties. As soon as one speaks of these things, there arises the deformation produced in the consciousness by all the social and moral conventions. As soon as you speak of purity, a moral monument comes in front of you which completely falsifies your notion. And note that it is infinitely easier to be moral from the social point of view than to be moral from the spiritual point of view. To be moral from the social viewpoint one has only to pay good attention to do nothing which is not approved of by others; this may be somewhat difficult, but still it is not impossible; and one may be, as I said, a monument of insincerity and impurity while doing this; whereas to be pure from the spiritual point of view means a vigilance, a consciousness, a sincerity that stand all tests.

Now, I may put you on your guard against something... about people who live in their vital consciousness and say, "I indeed am above moral laws, I follow a higher law, I am free from all moral laws." And they say this because they want to indulge in all irregularities. These people, then, have a double impurity: they have spiritual impurity and in addition social impurity. And these usually have a very good opinion of themselves, and they assert their wish to live their life with an unequalled impudence.

Yet usually the people whom I have found most difficult to convert are very respectable people. I am sorry, but I have had much more difficulty with respectable people than with those who were not so, for they had such a good opinion of themselves that it was impossible to open them. But the true thing *is* difficult. That is to say, one must be very vigilant and very self-controlled, very patient, and have a never-failing goodwill. One must not neglect having a small dose of humility, a sufficient one, and one must never be satisfied with the sincerity one has. One must always want more.

THE MOTHER

I have known people (many, not only a few, I mean among those who do yoga), I have known many who, every time they had a fine aspiration, and their aspiration was very strong and they received an answer to this aspiration, every time, the very same day or at the latest the next day, they had a complete setback of consciousness and were facing the exact opposite of their aspiration. Such things happen almost constantly. Well, these people have developed only the positive side. They make a kind of discipline of aspiration, they ask for help, they try to come into contact with higher forces, they succeed in this, they have experiences; but they have completely neglected cleaning their room; it has remained as dirty as ever, and so, naturally, when the experience has gone, this dirt becomes still more repulsive than before.

One must never neglect to clean one's room, it is very important; inner cleanliness is at least as important as outer cleanliness.

Vivekananda has written (I don't know the original, I have only read the French translation): "One must every morning clean one's soul and one's body, but if you don't have time for both, it is better to clean the soul than clean the body."

THE MOTHER

... you must never say: "I shall first purify my thought, purify my body, purify my vital and then later I shall purify my action." That is the normal order, but it never succeeds. The effective order is to begin from the outside: "The very first thing is that I do not do it, and afterwards, I desire it no longer and next I close my doors completely to all impulses: they no longer exist for me, I am now outside all that." This is the true order, the order that is effective. First, not to do it. And then you will no longer desire and after that it will go out of your consciousness completely.

THE MOTHER

Concentration

Along with purity and as a help to bring it about, concentration. Purity and concentration are indeed two aspects, feminine and masculine, passive and active, of the same status of being; purity is the condition in which concentration becomes entire, rightly effective, omnipotent; by concentration purity does its works and without it would only lead to a state of peaceful quiescence and eternal repose.... The fault of our nature is first an inert subjection to the impacts of things[1] as they come in upon the mind pell-mell without order or control and then a haphazard imperfect concentration managed fitfully, irregularly with a more or less chance emphasis on this or on that object according as they happen to interest, not the higher soul or the judging and discerning intellect, but the restless, leaping, fickle, easily tired, easily distracted lower mind which is the chief enemy of our progress. In such a condition purity, the right working of the functions, the clear, unstained and luminous order of the being is an impossibility; the various workings, given over to the chances of the environment and external influences, must necessarily run into each other and clog, divert, distract, pervert. Equally, without purity the complete, equal,

---

[1] *bāhyasparśa*

flexible concentration of the being in right thought, right will, right feeling or secure status of spiritual experience is not possible. Therefore the two must proceed together, each helping the victory of the other, until we arrive at that eternal calm from which may proceed some partial image in the human being of the eternal, omnipotent and omniscient activity.

SRI AUROBINDO

The mind is a thing that dwells in diffusion, in succession; it can only concentrate on one thing at a time and when not concentrated runs from one thing to another very much at random. Therefore it has to concentrate on a single idea, a single subject of meditation, a single object of contemplation, a single object of will in order to possess or master it, and this it must do to at least the temporary exclusion of all others.... The first step in concentration must be always to accustom the discursive mind to a settled unwavering pursuit of a single course of connected thought on a single subject and this it must do undistracted by all lures and alien calls on its attention. Such concentration is common enough in our ordinary life, but it becomes more difficult when we have to do it inwardly without any outward object or action on which to keep the mind; yet this inward concentration is what the seeker of knowledge must effect.

SRI AUROBINDO

... whatever you may want to do in life, one thing is absolutely indispensable and at the basis of *everything*, the capacity of concentrating the attention. If you are able to gather together the rays of attention and consciousness on one point and can maintain this concentration with a persistent will, *nothing* can resist it – whatever it may be, from the most material physical development to the highest spiritual one. But this discipline must be followed in a constant and, it may be said, imperturbable way; not that you should always be concentrated on the same thing – that's not what I mean, I mean learning to concentrate.

And materially, for studies, sports, all physical or mental development, it is absolutely indispensable. And the value of an individual is proportionate to the value of his attention.

And from the spiritual point of view it is still more important. There is *no* spiritual obstacle which can resist a penetrating power of concentration. For instance, the discovery of the psychic being, union with the inner Divine, opening to the higher spheres, *all* can be obtained by an intense and obstinate power of concentration – but one must learn how to do it.

There is nothing in the human or even in the super-human field, to which the power of concentration is not the key.

You can be the best athlete, you can be the best student, you can be an artistic, literary or scientific genius, you can be the greatest saint with that faculty. And everyone has in himself a tiny little beginning of it – it is given to everybody, but people do not cultivate it.

THE MOTHER

You have asked what is the discipline to be followed in

order to convert the mental seeking into a living spiritual experience. The first necessity is the practice of concentration of your consciousness within yourself. The ordinary human mind has an activity on the surface which veils the real Self. But there is another, a hidden consciousness within behind the surface, one in which we can become aware of the real Self and of a larger deeper truth of nature, can realise the Self and liberate and transform the nature. To quiet the surface mind and begin to live within is the object of this concentration.

SRI AUROBINDO

I read in the Conversations*: "Concentration alone will lead you to this goal." Should one increase the time of meditation?*

Concentration does not mean meditation; on the contrary, concentration is a state one must be in continuously, whatever the outer activity. By concentration I mean that all the energy, all the will, all the aspiration must be turned only towards the Divine and His integral realisation in our consciousness.

THE MOTHER

To keep constantly a concentrated and in-gathered attitude is more important than having fixed hours of meditation.

THE MOTHER

* *Conversations* (of the Mother), 1956

Equanimity and Peace

Equality means a quiet and unmoved mind and vital, it means not to be touched or disturbed by things that happen or things said or done to you, but to look at them with a straight look, free from the distortions created by personal feeling, and to try to understand what is behind them, why they happen, what is to be learnt from them, what is it in oneself which they are cast against and what inner profit or progress one can make out of them; it means self-mastery over the vital movements, – anger and sensitiveness and pride as well as desire and the rest, – not to let them get hold of the emotional being and disturb the inner peace, not to speak and act in the rush and impulsion of these things, always to act and speak out of a calm inner poise of the spirit. It is not easy to have this equality in any full perfect measure, but one should always try more and more to make it the basis of one's inner state and outer movements.

                                         SRI AUROBINDO

To be calm, undisturbed and quiet is not the first condition for sadhana but for siddhi. It is only a few people (very few, one, two, three, four in a hundred sadhaks) who can get it from the first. Most have to go through a long preparation before they can get anywhere near it. Even afterwards when they begin to feel the peace and calm, it takes time to establish it – they swing between peace and disturbance for a fairly long time until all parts of the nature have accepted the truth and the peace.

                                         SRI AUROBINDO

Quietness is when the mind or vital is not troubled, restless, drawn about by or crowded with thoughts and feelings. Especially when either is detached and looks at these as a surface movement, we say that the mind or vital is quiet.

Calmness is a more positive condition, not merely an absence of restlessness, over-activity or trouble. When there is a clear or great or strong tranquillity which nothing troubles or can trouble, then we say that calm is established.

SRI AUROBINDO

It is quite usual to feel an established peace in the inner being even if there is disturbance on the surface. In fact that is the usual condition of the yogi before he has attained the absolute *samatā* in all the being.

SRI AUROBINDO

It is true that through whatever is strongest in him a sadhak can most easily open to the Divine. But...peace is necessary for all; without peace and an increasing purity, even if one opens, one cannot receive perfectly all that comes down through the opening. Light too is necessary for all – without light one cannot take full advantage of all that comes down.

SRI AUROBINDO

It is in the peace behind and that "something truer" in you that you must learn to live and feel it to be yourself. You must regard the rest as not your real self, but only a flux of changing or recurring movements on the surface which are sure to go as the true self emerges.

SRI AUROBINDO

When the peace is deep or wide it is usually in the inner being. The outer parts do not ordinarily go beyond a certain measure of quietude – they get deep peace only when they are flooded with it from the inner being.

SRI AUROBINDO

They [peace and patience] go together. By having patience under all kinds of pressure you lay the foundations of peace.

SRI AUROBINDO

It [purity] is more a condition than a substance. Peace helps to purity – since in peace disturbing influences cease and the essence of purity is to respond only to the Divine Influence and not to have an affinity with other movements.

SRI AUROBINDO

If you get peace, then to clean the vital becomes easy. If you simply clean and clean and do nothing else, you go very slowly – for the vital gets dirty again and has to be cleaned a hundred times. The peace is something that is clean in itself, so to get it is a positive way of securing your object. To look for dirt only and clean is the negative way.

SRI AUROBINDO

One can go forward even if there is not peace – quietude and concentration are necessary. Peace is necessary for the higher states to develop.

SRI AUROBINDO

It is quite natural that at first there should be the condition of calm and peace only when you sit for concentration. What is important is that there should be this condition whenever you sit and the pressure for it always there. But at other times the result is at first only a certain mental quiet and freedom from thoughts. Afterwards when the condition of peace is quite settled in the inner being – for it is the inner into which you enter whenever you concentrate, then it begins to come out and control the outer, so that the calm and peace remain even when working, mixing with others, talking or other occupations. For then whatever the outer consciousness is doing, one feels the inner being calm within – indeed one feels the inner being as one's real self while the outer is something superficial through which the inner acts on life.

SRI AUROBINDO

Someone has asked me what I meant by these words:

"One must be calm."

It is obvious that when I tell someone, "Be calm", I mean many different things according to the person. But the first indispensable calm is mental quietude, for generally that is the one that's most lacking. When I tell someone,

"Be calm", I mean: Try not to have restless, excited, agitated thoughts; try to quieten your mind and to stop turning around in all your imaginations and observations and mental constructions.

One could justifiably add a question: You tell us "Be calm", but what should we do to be calm?... The answer is always more or less the same: you must first of all feel the need for it and want it, and then aspire, and then try! For trying, there are innumerable methods which have been prescribed and attempted by many. These methods are generally long, arduous, difficult; and many people get discouraged before reaching the goal, for, the more they try, the more do their thoughts start whirling around and becoming restless in their heads.

For each one the method is different, but *first* one must feel the need, for whatever reason it may be – whether because one is tired or because one is overstrained or because one truly wants to rise beyond the state one lives in – one must first understand, feel the need of this quietude, this peace in the mind. And then, afterwards, one may try out successively all the methods, known ones and new, to attain the result.

Now, one quickly realises that there is another quietude which is necessary, and even very urgently needed – this is vital quietude, that is to say, the absence of desire. Only, the vital when not sufficiently developed, as soon as it is told to keep quiet, either goes to sleep or goes on strike; it says, "Ah! no. Nothing doing! I won't go any farther. If you don't give me the sustenance I need, excitement, enthusiasm, desire, even passion, I prefer not to move and I won't do anything any longer." So there the problem becomes a little more delicate and perhaps even more difficult still; for surely, to fall from excitement into inertia is very far from being a progress! One must never mistake inertia or a somnolent passivity for calm.

Quietude is a very positive state; there is a positive peace which is not the opposite of conflict – an active peace, contagious, powerful, which controls and calms, which puts everything in order, organises. It is of this I am speaking; when I tell someone, "Be calm", I don't mean to say "Go and sleep, be inert and passive, and don't do anything", far from it!... True quietude is a very great force, a very great strength. In fact one can say, looking at the problem from the other side, that all those who are really strong, powerful, are always very calm. It is only the weak who are agitated; as soon as one becomes truly strong, one is peaceful, calm, quiet, and one has the power of endurance to face the adverse waves which come rushing from outside in the hope of disturbing one. This true quietude is always a sign of force. Calmness belongs to the strong.

And this is true even in the physical field. I don't know if you have observed animals like lions, tigers, elephants, but it is a fact that when they are not in action, they are always so perfectly still. A lion sitting and looking at you always seems to be telling you, "Oh, how fidgety you are!" It looks at you with such a peaceful air of wisdom! And all its power, energy, physical strength are there, gathered, collected, concentrated and – without a shadow of agitation – ready for action when the order is given.

I have seen people, many people, who could not sit still for half an hour without fidgeting. They had to move a foot or a leg, or an arm or their head; they had to stir restlessly all the time, for they did not have the power or the strength to remain quiet.

This capacity to remain still when one wants to, to gather all one's energies and spend them as one wishes, completely if one wants, or to apportion them as one wants in action, with a perfect calm even in action – that is always the sign of strength. It may be physical strength or vital strength or mental strength. But if you are in the least agitated, you may be sure there is a weakness somewhere; and if your restlessness is integral, it is an integral weakness.

So, if I tell someone "Be calm", I may be telling him all kinds of things, it depends upon each person. But obviously, most often it is, "Make your mind quiet, don't be restless all the time in your head, don't stir up lots of ideas, calm yourself."

THE MOTHER

How can we establish a settled peace and silence in the mind?

First of all, you must want it.

And then you must try and must persevere, continue trying. What I have just told you is a very good means. Yet there are others also. You sit quietly, to begin with; and then, instead of thinking of fifty things, you begin saying to yourself, "Peace, peace, peace, peace, peace, calm, peace!" You imagine peace and calm. You aspire, ask that it may come: "Peace, peace, calm." And then, when something comes and touches you and acts, say quietly, like this, "Peace, peace, peace." Do not look at the thoughts, do not listen to the thoughts, you understand. You must not pay attention to everything that comes. You know, when someone bothers you a great deal and you want to get rid of him, you don't listen to him, do you? Good! You turn your head away (*gesture*) and think of something else. Well, you must do that: when thoughts come, you must not look at them, must not listen to them, must not pay any attention at all. You must behave as though they did not exist, you see! And then, repeat all the time like a kind of – how shall I put it? – as an idiot does, who repeats the same thing always. Well, you must do the same thing; you must repeat, "Peace, peace, peace." So you try this for a few minutes and then do what you have to do; and then, another time, you begin again; sit down again and then try. Do this on getting up in the morning, do this in the evening when going to bed. You can do this... look, if you want to digest your food properly, you can do this for a few minutes before eating. You can't imagine how much this helps your digestion! Before beginning to eat you sit quietly for a while and say, "Peace, peace, peace!" and *everything* becomes calm. It seems as though all the noises were going far, far, far away (*Mother stretches out her arms on both sides*) and then you must continue; and there comes a time when you no longer need to sit down, and no matter what you are doing, no matter what you are saying, it is always "Peace, peace, peace." Everything remains here, like this, it does not enter (*gesture in front of the forehead*), it remains like this. And then one is always in a perfect peace... after some years.

But at the beginning, a very small beginning, two or three minutes, it is very simple. For something complicated you must make an effort, and when one makes an effort, one is not quiet. It is difficult to make an effort while remaining quiet. Very simple, very simple, you must be very simple in these things. It is as though you were learning how to call a friend: by dint of being called he comes. Well, make peace and calm your friends and call them: "Come, peace, peace, peace, peace, come!"

THE MOTHER

V

GROWTH OF CONSCIOUSNESS
MEANS AND METHODS

... men differ in nature and therefore each will approach the sadhana in his own way – one through work, one through bhakti, one through meditation and knowledge – and those who are capable of it, through all together. You are perfectly justified in following your own way, whatever may be the theories of others – but let them follow theirs. In the end all can converge together towards the same goal.

SRI AUROBINDO

In various times and places many methods have been prescribed for attaining this perception and ultimately achieving this identification. Some methods are psychological, some religious, some even mechanical. In reality, everyone has to find the one which suits him best, and if one has an ardent and steadfast aspiration, a persistent and dynamic will, one is sure to meet, in one way or another – outwardly through reading and study, inwardly through concentration, meditation, revelation and experience – the help one needs to reach the goal.

THE MOTHER

GROWTH OF CONSCIOUSNESS
MEANS AND METHODS

Many Methods

What is the difference between mechanical, religious and psychological methods? Religious methods are those adopted by the various religions. Not many religions speak of the inner Truth; for them, it is more a matter of coming into contact with their God. Heaven and hell: this is a roundabout way of saying...*

Psychological methods are those that deal with states of consciousness, that try to realise the inner self by withdrawing from all activity and attempting to create the conscious inner conditions of detachment, self-abstraction, concentration, higher Reality, renunciation of all the outer movements, etc. A psychological method is one which acts on the thoughts, feelings and actions.

Mechanical methods are those which are based on purely mechanical means – one can benefit from them by using them in a certain way. Take breath-control, for example: it acts more or less mechanically, but it is sometimes recommended to add to this a concentration of one's thought, to repeat a word, as in Vivekananda's teaching. This works up to a certain point, but then it fades away. These human attempts in various times and places have been more or less successful individually but they have never given a collective result.

The psychological method is far more difficult but far more effective: through your actions, to be in a state of

---

* Words missing in the transcription.

inner will to express nothing in yourself but the Truth of your being, and to make everything dependent on that Truth. Of course, if you do nothing, it is easier, but it is also easier to deceive yourself. When you sit down in isolation, in complete silence and far away from everybody, and examine yourself with more or less indulgent eyes, you may imagine that you are realising something wonderful. But when you are put to the test at every minute of your life, when you have the occasion to become aware of your imperfections, your infirmities, your little movements of bad will a hundred times a day, you soon lose the illusion of being...* and so your efforts are more sincere.

THE MOTHER

The growth out of the ordinary mind into the spiritual consciousness can be effected either by meditation, dedicated work or bhakti for the Divine.

SRI AUROBINDO

The object of the sadhana is opening of the consciousness to the Divine and the change of the nature. Meditation or contemplation is one means to this but only one means; bhakti is another; work is another.

SRI AUROBINDO

Work, bhakti and meditation are the three supports of

---

* Words missing in the transcription.

yoga. One can do with all three or two or one. There are people who can't meditate in the set way that one calls meditation, but they progress through work or through bhakti or through the two together. By work and bhakti one can develop a consciousness in which eventually a natural meditation and realisation becomes possible.

SRI AUROBINDO

Meditation

There are two words used in English to express the Indian idea of *dhyāna*, "meditation" and "contemplation". Meditation means properly the concentration of the mind on a single train of ideas which work out a single subject. Contemplation means regarding mentally a single object, image, idea so that the knowledge about the object, image or idea may arise naturally in the mind by force of the concentration. Both these things are forms of *dhyāna*, for the principle of *dhyāna* is mental concentration whether in thought, vision or knowledge.

There are other forms of *dhyāna*. There is a passage in which Vivekananda advises you to stand back from your thoughts, let them occur in your mind as they will and simply observe them and see what they are. This may be called concentration in self-observation.

This form leads to another, the emptying of all thought out of the mind so as to leave it a sort of pure vigilant blank on which the divine knowledge may come and imprint itself, undisturbed by the inferior thoughts of the ordinary human mind and with the clearness of a writing in white chalk on a blackboard. You will find that the Gita speaks of this rejection of all mental thought as one of the methods of yoga and even the method it seems to prefer. This may be called the *dhyāna* of liberation, as it frees the mind from slavery to the mechanical process of thinking and allows it to think or not to think, as it pleases and when it pleases, or to choose its own thoughts or else to go beyond thought to the pure perception of Truth called in our philosophy *Vijñāna*.

Meditation is the easiest process for the human mind, but the narrowest in its results; contemplation more difficult, but greater; self-observation and liberation from the chains of Thought the most difficult of all, but the widest and greatest in its fruits. One can choose any of them according to one's bent and capacity. The perfect method is to use them all, each in its own place and for its own object; but this would need a fixed faith and firm patience and a great energy of Will in the self-application to the yoga.

SRI AUROBINDO

Conditions internal and external that are most essential for meditation.

There are no *essential* external condtions, but solitude and seclusion at the time of meditation as well as stillness of the body are helpful, sometimes almost necessary to the beginner. But one should not be bound by external conditions. Once the habit of meditation is formed, it should be made possible to do it in all circumstances, lying, sitting, walking, alone, in company, in silence or in the midst of noise etc.

The first internal condition necessary is concentration of the will against the obstacles to meditation, i.e. wandering of the mind, forgetfulness, sleep, physical and nervous impatience and restlessness etc.

The second is an increasing purity and calm of the inner consciousness (*citta*) out of which thought and emotion arise, i.e. a freedom from all disturbing reactions, such as anger, grief, depression, anxiety about worldly happenings etc. Mental perfection and moral are always closely allied to each other.

SRI AUROBINDO

The sitting motionless posture is the natural posture for concentrated meditation – walking and standing are active conditions. It is only when one has gained the enduring rest and passivity of the consciousness that it is easy to concentrate and receive when walking or doing anything. A fundamental passive condition of the consciousness gathered into itself is the proper poise for concentration and a seated gathered immobility in the body is the best position for that. It can be done also lying down, but that position is too passive, tending to be inert rather than gathered. This is the reason why yogis always sit in an *āsana*. One can accustom oneself to meditate walking, standing, lying but sitting is the first natural position.

SRI AUROBINDO

What does Sri Aurobindo mean by "a self-dynamising meditation"?

It is a meditation that has the power of transforming your being. It is a meditation which makes you progress, as opposed to static meditation which is immobile and relatively inert, and which changes nothing in your consciousness or in your way of being. A dynamic meditation is a meditation of transformation.

Generally, people don't have a dynamic meditation. When they enter into meditation – or at least what they call meditation – they enter into a kind of immobility where nothing stirs, and they come out of it exactly as they went in, without any change either in their being or in their consciousness. And the more motionless it is, the happier they are. They could meditate in this way for eternities, it would never change anything either in the universe or in themselves. That is why Sri Aurobindo speaks of a dynamic meditation which is exactly the very opposite. It is a transforming meditation.

How is it done? Is it done in a different way?

I think it is the aspiration that should be different, the attitude should be different. "Different way" – what do you mean by "way" – (*laughing*) the way of sitting?... Not that? The inner way?

Yes.

But for each one it is different.

I think the most important thing is to know why one meditates; this is what gives the quality of the meditation and makes it of one order or another.

You may meditate to open yourself to the divine Force,

you may meditate to reject the ordinary consciousness, you may meditate to enter the depths of your being, you may meditate to learn how to give yourself integrally; you may meditate for all kinds of things. You may meditate to enter into peace and calm and silence – this is what people generally do, but without much success. But you may also meditate to receive the Force of transformation, to discover the points to be transformed, to trace out the line of progress. And then you may also meditate for very practical reasons: when you have a difficulty to clear up, a solution to find, when you want help in some action or other. You may meditate for that too.

I think everyone has his own mode of meditation. But if one wants the meditation to be dynamic, one must have an aspiration for progress and the meditation must be done to help and fulfil this aspiration for progress. Then it becomes dynamic.

THE MOTHER

One can have no fixed hours of meditation and yet be doing sadhana.

SRI AUROBINDO

Concentration is a gathering together of the consciousness and either centralising at one point or turning on a single object, e.g., the Divine; there can also be a gathered condition throughout the whole being, not at a point. In meditation it is not indispensable to gather like this, one can simply remain with a quiet mind thinking of one subject or observing what comes in the consciousness and dealing with it.

SRI AUROBINDO

Concentration means fixing the consciousness in one place or on one object and in a single condition. Meditation can be diffusive, e.g., thinking about the Divine, receiving impressions and discriminating, watching what goes on in the nature and acting upon it, etc.

SRI AUROBINDO

Ordinarily the consciousness is spread out everywhere, dispersed, running in this or that direction, after this subject and that object in multitude. When anything has to be done of a sustained nature the first thing one does is to draw back all this dispersed consciousness and concentrate. It is then, if one looks closely, bound to be concentrated in one place and on one occupation, subject or object – as when you are composing a poem or a botanist is studying a flower. The place is usually somewhere in the brain if it is the thought, in the heart if it is the feeling in which one is concentrated. The yogic concentration is simply an extension and intensification of the same thing. It may be on an object as when one does Tratak on a shining point – then one has to concentrate so that one sees only that point and has no other thought than that. It may be on an idea or word or a name, the idea of the Divine, the word OM, the name Krishna, or a combination of idea and word or idea and name. But further in yoga one also concentrates in a particular place. There is the famous rule of concentrating between the eyebrows – the centre of the inner mind, of occult vision, of the will is there. What you do is to think firmly from there on whatever you make the object of your concentration or else try to see the image of it from there. If you succeed in this then after a time you feel that your whole consciousness is centred there in that place – of course for the time being. After doing it for some time and often it becomes easy and normal....

It may be asked what becomes of the rest of the consciousness when there is this local concentration? Well, it either falls silent as in any concentration or, if it does not, then thoughts or other things may move about, as if outside, but the concentrated part does not attend to them or notice. That is when the concentration is reasonably successful.

One has not to fatigue oneself at first by long concentration if one is not accustomed, for then in a jaded mind it loses its power and value. One can relax and meditate instead of concentrating. It is only as the concentration becomes normal that one can go on for a longer and longer time.

SRI AUROBINDO

If one concentrates on a thought or a word, one has to dwell on the essential idea contained in the word with the aspiration to feel the thing which it expresses.

SRI AUROBINDO

There is no harm in concentrating sometimes in the heart and sometimes above the head. But concentration in either place does not mean keeping the attention fixed on a particular spot; you have to take your station of consciousness in either place and concentrate there not on the place, but on the Divine. This can be done with eyes shut or with eyes open, according as it best suits you.

SRI AUROBINDO

The mind is always in activity, but we do not observe fully what it is doing, but allow ourselves to be carried away in the stream of continual thinking. When we try to concentrate, this stream of self-made mechanical thinking becomes prominent to our observation. It is the first normal obstacle (the other is sleep during meditation) to the effort for yoga.

The best thing to do is to realise that the thought-flow is not yourself, it is not you who are thinking, but thought that is going on in the mind. It is Prakriti with its thought-energy that is raising all this whirl of thought in you, imposing it on the Purusha. You as the Purusha must stand back as the witness observing the action, but refusing to identify yourself with it. The next thing is to exercise a control and reject the thoughts – though sometimes by the very act of detachment the thought-habit falls away or diminishes during the meditation and there is a sufficient silence or at any rate a quietude which makes it easy to reject the thoughts that come and fix oneself on the object of meditation. If one becomes aware of the thoughts as coming from outside, from the universal Nature, then one can throw them out before they reach the mind; in that way the mind finally falls silent. If neither of these things happens, a persistent practice of rejection becomes necessary – there should be no struggle or wrestling with the thought, but only a quiet self-separation and refusal. Success does not come at first, but if consent is constantly withheld, the mechanical whirl eventually ceases and begins to die away and one can then have at will an inner quietude or silence.

It should be noted that the result of the yogic processes is not, except in rare cases, immediate and one must apply the will-patience till they give a result which is sometimes long in coming if there is much resistance in the outer nature.

Sri Aurobindo

Work

There are some people who are not cut out for meditation and it is only by work that they can prepare themselves; there are also those who are the opposite.

Sri Aurobindo

The including of the outer consciousness in the transformation is of supreme importance in this yoga – meditation cannot do it. Meditation can deal only with the inner being. So work is of primary importance – only it must be done with the right attitude and in the right consciousness, then it is as fruitful as any meditation can be.

Sri Aurobindo

… that is one great utility of work that it tests the nature and puts the sadhak in front of the defects of his outer being which might otherwise escape him.

Sri Aurobindo

To keep up work helps to keep up the balance between the internal experience and the external development; otherwise one-sidedness and want of measure and balance may develop. Moreover, it is necessary to keep the sadhana of work for the Divine because in the end that enables the sadhak to bring out the inner progress into the external nature and life and helps the integrality of the sadhana.

SRI AUROBINDO

It may be necessary for an individual here and there to plunge into meditation for a time and suspend work for that time or make it subordinate; but that can only be an individual case and a temporary retirement. Moreover, a complete cessation of work and entire withdrawal into oneself is seldom advisable; it may encourage a too one-sided and visionary condition in which one lives in a sort of mid-world of purely subjective experiences without a firm hold on either external reality or on the highest Reality and without the right use of the subjective experience to create a firm link and then a unification between the highest Reality and the external realisation in life.

SRI AUROBINDO

I do not mean by work action done in the ego and the ignorance, for the satisfaction of the ego and in the drive of rajasic desire. There can be no Karmayoga without the will to get rid of ego, rajas and desire, which are the seals of ignorance.

I do not mean philanthropy or the service of humanity

or all the rest of the things – moral or idealistic – which the mind of man substitutes for the deeper truth of works.

I mean by work action done for the Divine and more and more in union with the Divine – for the Divine alone and nothing else. Naturally that is not easy at the beginning, any more than deep meditation and luminous knowledge are easy or even true love and bhakti are easy. But like the others it has to be begun in the right spirit and attitude, with the right will in you, then all the rest will come.

SRI AUROBINDO

The ordinary life consists in work for personal aim and satisfaction of desire under some mental or moral control, touched sometimes by a mental ideal. The Gita's yoga consists in the offering of one's work as a sacrifice to the Divine, the conquest of desire, egoless and desireless action....

SRI AUROBINDO

... the Gita is the great guide on this path. Purification from egoistic movements and from personal desire and the faithful following of the best light one has are a preliminary training for this path....

SRI AUROBINDO

The first step in Karmayoga of this kind is to diminish and finally get rid of the ego-centric position in works, the lower vital reactions and the principle of desire.

SRI AUROBINDO

Any work can be done as a field for the practice of the spirit of the Gita.

SRI AUROBINDO

Men usually work and carry on their affairs from the ordinary motives of the vital being, need, desire of wealth or success or position or power or fame or the push to activity and the pleasure of manifesting their capacities, and they succeed or fail according to their capability, power of work and the good or bad fortune which is the result of their nature and their Karma. When one takes up the yoga and wishes to consecrate one's life to the Divine, these ordinary motives of the vital being have no longer their full and free play; they have to be replaced by another, a mainly psychic and spiritual motive, which will enable the sadhak to work with the same force as before, no longer for himself, but for the Divine.

SRI AUROBINDO

The only work that spiritually purifies is that which is done without personal motives, without desire for fame or public recognition or worldly greatness, without insistence on one's own mental motives or vital lusts and demands or physical preferences, without vanity or crude self-assertion or claim for position or prestige, done for the sake of the Divine alone.... All work done in an egoistic spirit, however good for people in the world of the Ignorance, is of no avail to the seeker of the yoga.

SRI AUROBINDO

All should be done quietly from within – working, speaking, reading, writing as part of the real consciousness – not with the dispersed and unquiet movement of the ordinary consciousness.

SRI AUROBINDO

Of course the idea of bigness and smallness is quite foreign to the spiritual truth.... Spiritually there is nothing big or small. Such ideas are like those of the literary people who think writing a poem is a high work and making shoes or cooking the dinner is a small and low one. But all is equal in the eyes of the Spirit – and it is only the spirit within with which it is done that matters. It is the same with a particular kind of work, there is nothing big or small.

SRI AUROBINDO

"If a division of works has to be made, it is between those that are nearest to the heart of the sacred flame and those that are least touched or illumined by it because they are more at a distance, or between the fuel that burns strongly or brightly and the logs that if too thickly heaped on the altar may impede the ardour of the fire by their damp, heavy and diffused abundance." SRI AUROBINDO

(*The Synthesis of Yoga*, Centenary Library, Vol. 20, p. 132)

Psychologically, to what does this division correspond in our life?

I suppose it is different for each one. So each one must find those activities which increase his aspiration, his consciousness, his deeper knowledge of things, and those which, on the contrary, mechanise him and bring him back more thoroughly into a purely material relation with things.

It is difficult to make a general rule.

> *That means that everything ought to be done exactly, as an offering?*

Truly speaking, it depends more on the way of doing a thing than on the thing itself.

You take up some work which is quite material, like cleaning the floor or dusting a room; well, it seems to me that this work can lead to a very deep consciousness if it is done with a certain feeling for perfection and progress; while other work considered of a higher kind as, for example, studies or literary and artistic work, if done with the idea of seeking fame or for the satisfaction of one's vanity or for some material gain, will not help you to progress. So this is already a kind of classification which depends more on the inner attitude than on the outer fact. But this classification can be applied to everything.

Of course, there is a kind of work which is done only for purely pecuniary and personal reasons, like the one – whatever it may be – which is done to earn a living. That attitude is exactly the one Sri Aurobindo compares with the damp logs of wood which are heaped so thick the flame cannot leap up. It has something dark and heavily dull about it.

THE MOTHER

It is not that you have to do what you dislike, but that you have to cease to dislike. To do only what you like is to indulge the vital and maintain its domination over the nature – for that is the very principle of the untransformed nature, to be governed by its likes and dislikes. To be able to do anything with equanimity is the principle of Karmayoga....

SRI AUROBINDO

It depends on a certain extension and intensifying of the consciousness by which all activity becomes interesting not for itself but because of the consciousness put into it and, through the intensity of the energy, there is a pleasure in the exercise of the energy, and in the perfect doing of the work, whatever the work may be.

SRI AUROBINDO

... one of the two ways towards yoga by works is the separation of the Purusha from the Prakriti, the inner silent being from the outer active one, so that one has two consciousnesses or a double consciousness, one behind watching and observing and finally controlling and changing the other which is active in front. But this also means living in an inner peace and silence and dealing with the activities as if they were a thing of the surface. The other way of beginning the yoga of works is by doing them for the Divine, for the Mother, and not for oneself, consecrating and dedicating them till one concretely feels the Divine Force taking up the activities and doing them for one.

SRI AUROBINDO

It is easy for one, comparatively, to remember and be conscious when one sits quiet in meditation; it is difficult when one has to be busy with work. The remembrance and consciousness in work have to come by degrees, you must not expect to have it all at once; nobody can get it all at once. It comes in two ways, – first, if one practises remembering the Mother and offering the work to her each time one does something (not all the time one is doing, but at the beginning or whenever one can remember,) then that slowly becomes easy and habitual to the nature. Secondly, by the meditation an inner consciousness begins to develop which, after a time, not at once or suddenly, becomes more and more automatically permanent. One feels this as a separate consciousness from that outer which works. At first this separate consciousness is not felt when one is working, but as soon as the work stops one feels it was there all the time watching from behind; afterwards it begins to be felt during the work itself, as if there were two parts of oneself – one watching and supporting from behind and remembering the Mother and offering to her and the other doing the work. When this happens, then to work with the true consciousness becomes more and more easy.

                                          SRI AUROBINDO

A time comes for the sadhak in the end when the consciousness and the deeper experience go on happening even in full work or in sleep, while speaking or in any kind of activity.

                                          SRI AUROBINDO

To say that one enters the stream of sadhana through work only is to say too much. One can enter it through meditation or bhakti also, but work is necessary to get into full stream and not drift away to one side and go circling there. Of course all work helps provided it is done in the right spirit.

Sri Aurobindo

Work done in the true spirit is meditation.

The Mother

Bhakti – Devotion

There is always the personal and the impersonal side of the Divine and the Truth and it is a mistake to think the impersonal alone to be true or important, for that leads to a void incompleteness in part of the being, while only one side is given satisfaction. Impersonality belongs to the intellectual mind and the static self, personality to the soul and heart and dynamic being. Those who disregard the personal Divine ignore something which is profound and essential.

In following the heart in its purer impulses one follows something that is at least as precious as the mind's loyalty to its own conceptions of what the Truth may be.

Sri Aurobindo

The nature of Bhakti is adoration, worship, self-offering to what is greater than oneself....

Bhakti is not an experience, it is a state of the heart and soul. It is a state which comes when the psychic being is awake and prominent.

SRI AUROBINDO

Prayer and meditation count for so much in yoga. But the prayer must well up from the heart on a crest of emotion or aspiration, the Japa or meditation come in a live push carrying the joy or the light of the thing in it. If done mechanically and merely as a thing that ought to be done (stern grim duty!), it must tend towards want of interest and dryness and so be ineffective....

SRI AUROBINDO

What is meant by *bāhyapūjā* [external worship]? If it is purely external, then of course it is the lowest form; but if done with the true consciousness, it can bring the greatest possible completeness to the adoration by allowing the body and the most external consciousness to share in the spirit and act of worship.

SRI AUROBINDO

... the deeper the emotion, the more intense the Bhakti, the greater is the force for realisation and transformation. It is oftenest through intensity of emotion that the psychic being awakes and there is an opening of the inner doors to the Divine.

SRI AUROBINDO

The very object of yoga is a change of consciousness – it is by getting a new consciousness or by unveiling the hidden consciousness of the true being within and progressively manifesting and perfecting it that one gets first the contact and then the union with the Divine. Ananda and Bhakti are part of that deeper consciousness, and it is only when one lives in it and grows in it that Ananda and Bhakti can be permanent. Till then, one can only get experiences of Ananda and Bhakti, but not the constant and permanent state. But the state of Bhakti and constantly growing surrender does not come to all at an early stage of the sadhana; many, most indeed, have a long journey of purification and Tapasya to go through before it opens, and experiences of this kind, at first rare and interspersed, afterwards frequent, are the landmarks of their progress. It depends on certain conditions, which have nothing to do with superior or inferior yoga-capacity, but rather with a predisposition in the heart to open, as you say, to the Sun of the Divine Influence.

SRI AUROBINDO

Following One's Own Path

Everyone must follow his path in accordance with his own nature, and there is always a preference for one way rather than another... for one who follows the path of action, it is much more difficult to feel that the human personality does not exist and that only the divine Force works. For one who follows the path of knowledge it is relatively very easy, it is something one discovers almost immediately. For one who follows the path of love it is elementary, since it is by giving himself that he progresses. But for one who follows the path of action it is much more difficult, and consequently for him the first step is to do what is said here in the passage of *The Synthesis of Yoga* which we have just read*: to create in himself this complete detachment from the fruit of action, to act because this is what must be done, to do it in the best possible way, and not to be anxious about the consequences, to leave the consequences to a Will higher than his own.

---

* "It is then by a transformation of life in its very principle, not by an external manipulation of its phenomena, that the integral Yoga proposes to change it from a troubled and ignorant into a luminous and harmonious movement of Nature. There are three conditions which are indispensable for the achievement of this central inner revolution and a new formation; none of them is altogether sufficient in itself, but by their united threefold power the uplifting can be done, the conversion made and completely made. For, first, life as it is is a movement of desire and it has built in us as its centre a desire-soul which refers to itself all the motions of life and puts in them its own troubled hue and pain of an ignorant, half-lit, baffled endeavour: for a divine living, desire must be abolished and replaced by a purer and firmer motive-power, the tormented soul of desire dissolved and in its stead there must emerge the calm, strength, happiness of a true vital being now concealed within us. Next, life as it is is driven or led partly by the impulse of the life-force, partly by a mind which is mostly a servant and abettor of the ignorant life-impulse, but in part also its uneasy and not too luminous or competent guide and mentor; for a divine life the mind and the life-impulse must cease to be anything but instruments and the inmost psychic being must take their place as the leader on the path and the indicator of a divine guidance. Last, life as it is is turned towards the satisfaction of the separative ego; ego must disappear and be replaced by the true spiritual person, the central being, and life itself must be turned towards the fulfilment of the Divine in terrestrial existence; it must feel a Divine Force awaking within it and become an obedient instrumentation of its purpose." – Sri Aurobindo

(*The Synthesis of Yoga*, Centenary Library, Vol. 20, p. 166)

One can't make a general rule for the order of importance of the paths, it is an exclusively personal affair. And
there is a time when one understands very well, it is
apparent, that no two paths are alike, no two paths can be
alike, and that every man follows his own path and that
this is the truth of his being. One can, if one looks from a
sufficient height, see a difference in the speed of advance,
but it does not always conform to the external signs; and
one could say a little humorously, that it is not always the
wisest who goes fastest!

THE MOTHER

Each mind can have its own way of approaching the
supreme Truth and there is an entrance for each as well as
a thousand ways for the journey to it. It is not necessary to
believe in the Grace or to recognise a Godhead different
from one's highest Self – there are ways of yoga that do
not accept these things. Also, for many no form of yoga is
necessary – they arrive at some realisation by a sort of
pressure of the mind or the heart or the will breaking the
screen between it and what is at once beyond it and its
own source. What happens after the breaking of the
screen depends on the play of the Truth on the consciousness and the turn of the nature. There is no reason,
therefore, why X's realisation of his being should not
come in its own way by growth from within, not by the
Divine Grace, if his mind objects to that description, but,
let us say, by the spontaneous movement of the Self within
him.

For, as to this "Grace", we describe it in that way
because we feel in the infinite Spirit or Self-existence a

Presence or a Being, a Consciousness that determines, – that is what we speak of as the Divine, – not a separate person, but the one Being of whom our individual self is a portion or a vessel. But it is not necessary for everybody to regard it in that way. Supposing it is the impersonal Self of all only, yet the Upanishad says of this Self and its realisation: "This understanding is not to be gained by reasoning nor by tapasya nor by much learning, but whom this Self chooses, to him it reveals its own body". Well, that is the same thing as what we call the Divine Grace, – it is an action from above or from within independent of mental causes which decides its own movement. We can call it the Divine Grace; we can call it the Self within choosing its own hour and way to manifest to the mental instrument on the surface; we can call it the flowering of the inner being or inner nature into self-realisation and self-knowledge. As something in us approaches it or as it presents itself to us, so the mind sees it. But in reality it is the same thing and the same process of the being in Nature.

SRI AUROBINDO

VI

GROWTH OF CONSCIOUSNESS
DIFFICULTIES AND PITFALLS

All who enter the spiritual path have to face the difficulties and ordeals of the path, those which rise from their own nature and those which come in from outside. The difficulties in the nature always rise again and again till you overcome them; they must be faced with both strength and patience....

All who cleave to the path steadfastly can be sure of their spiritual destiny. If anyone fails to reach it, it can only be for one of the two reasons, either because they leave the path or because for some lure of ambition, vanity, desire, etc. they go astray....

SRI AUROBINDO

GROWTH OF CONSCIOUSNESS
DIFFICULTIES AND PITFALLS

Human nature and the character of the individual are a formation that has arisen in and out of the inconscience of the material world and can never get entirely free from the pressure of that Inconscience. As consciousness grows in the being born into this material world, it takes the form of an Ignorance slowly admitting or striving with difficulty after knowledge and human nature is made of that Ignorance and the character of the individual is made from the elements of the Ignorance. It is largely mechanistic like everything else in material Nature and there is almost invariably a resistance and, more often than not, a strong and stubborn resistance to any change demanded from it. The character is made up of habits and it clings to them, is disposed to think them the very law of its being and it is a hard job to get it to change at all except under a strong pressure of circumstances. Especially in the physical parts, the body, the physical mind, the physical life movements, there is this resistance; the tamasic element in Nature is powerful there, what the Gita describes as *aprakāśa*, absence of light, and *apravṛtti*, a tendency to inertia, inactivity, unwillingness to make an effort and, as a result, even when the effort is made, a constant readiness to doubt, to despond and despair, to give up, renounce the aim and the endeavour, collapse. Fortunately, there is also in human nature a sattwic element which turns towards light and a rajasic or kinetic element which desires and needs to act and can be made to desire not only change but constant progress. But these too, owing to the limitations of human ignorance and the obstructions of the fundamental inconscience, suffer from pettiness and division and can resist as well as assist the spiritual endeavour. The spiritual change which yoga demands from human nature and individual character is, therefore, full of difficulties, one may almost say that it is the most difficult of all human aspirations and efforts. In so far as it can get the sattwic and the rajasic (kinetic) elements to assist it, its path is made easier but even the sattwic element can resist by attachment to old ideas, to preconceived notions, to mental preferences and partial judgments, to opinions and reasonings which come in the way of higher truth and to which it is attached: the kinetic element resists by its egoism, its passions, desires and strong attachments, its vanity and self-esteem, its constant habit of demand and many other obstacles. The resistance of the vital has a more violent character than the others and it brings to the aid of the others its own violence and passion and that is a source of all the acute difficulty, revolt, upheavals and disorders which mar the course of the yoga. The Divine is there, but He does not ignore the conditions, the laws, the circumstances of Nature; it is under these conditions that He does all His work, His work in the world and in man and consequently also in the sadhak, the aspirant, even in the God-knower and God-lover; even the saint and the sage continue to have difficulties and to be limited by their human nature. A complete liberation and a complete perfection or the complete possession of the Divine and possession by the Divine is possible, but it does not usually happen by an easy miracle or a series of miracles. The miracle can and does happen but only when there is the full call and complete self-giving of the soul and the entire widest opening of the nature.

Still, if the call of the soul is there, although not yet full, however great and obstinate the difficulties, there can be no final and irretrievable failure; even when the thread is broken, it is taken up again and reunited and carried to its end. There is a working in the nature itself in response to the inner need which, however slowly, brings about the result.

SRI AUROBINDO

Yoga has always its difficulties, whatever yoga it be. Moreover, it acts in a different way on different seekers. Some have to overcome the difficulties of their nature first before they get any experiences to speak of, others get a splendid beginning and all the difficulties afterwards, others go on for a long time having alternate risings to the top of the wave and then a descent into the gulfs and so on till the difficulty is worked out, others have a smooth path which does not mean that they have no difficulties – they have plenty, but they do not care a straw for them, because they feel that the Divine will help them to the goal or that he is with them even when they do not feel him – their faith makes them imperturbable.

SRI AUROBINDO

I have never said that yoga or that this yoga is a safe and easy path. What I say is that anyone who has the will to go through, can go through. For the rest, if you aim high there is always the danger of a steep fall if you misconduct your aeroplane. But the danger is for those who allow themselves to entertain a double being, aiming high but also indulging their lower outlook and hankerings. What else can you expect when people do that? You must become single-minded, then the difficulties of the mind and vital will be overcome. Otherwise, those who oscillate between their heights and their abysses will always be in danger till they have become single-minded. That applies to the "advanced" as well as to the beginner. These are facts of nature; I can't pretend for anybody's comfort that they are otherwise. But there is the fact also that nobody need keep himself in this danger. One-mindedness, surrender to the Divine, faith, true love for the Divine, complete sincerity in the will, spiritual humility (real, not formal) – there are so many things that can be a safeguard against any chance of eventual downfall. Slips, stumbles, difficulties, upsettings everyone has; one can't be assured against these things, but if one has the safeguards, they are transitory, help the nature to learn and are followed by a better progress.

SRI AUROBINDO

The difficulty is that in everyone there are two people (to say the least) – one in the outer vital and physical clinging to the past self and trying to get or retain the consent of the mind and the inner being, the other which is the soul asking for a new birth. That which has spoken in you and made the prayer is the psychic being expressing itself through the aid of the mind and the higher vital, and it is this which should always arise in you through prayer and through turning to the Mother and give you the right idea and the right impulse.

It is true that if you refuse always the action suggested by the old Adam, it will be a great step forward. The struggle is then transferred to the psychological plane, where it will be much easier to fight the matter out. I do not deny that there will be difficulty for some time; but if there is the control of action, the control of thought and feeling is bound to come. If there is yielding, on the contrary, a fresh lease is given to the old self.

SRI AUROBINDO

... the experience which so alarms you, of states of consciousness in which you say and do things contrary to your true will, is not a reason for despair. It is a common experience in one form or another of all who try to rise above their ordinary nature. Not only those who practise yoga, but religious men and even those who seek only a moral control and self-improvement are confronted with this difficulty. And here again it is not the yoga or the effort after perfection that creates this condition, – there are contradictory elements in human nature and in every human being through which he is made to act in a way which his better mind disapproves. This happens to everybody, to the most ordinary men in the most ordinary life. It only becomes marked and obvious to our minds when we try to rise above our ordinary external selves, because then we can see that it is the lower elements which are being made to revolt consciously against the higher will. There then seems to be for a time a division in the nature, because the true being and all that supports it stand back and separate from these lower elements. At one time the true being occupies the field of the nature, at another the lower nature used by some contrary Force pushes it back and seizes the ground.... If there is the firm will to progress, this division is overpassed and in the unified nature, unified around that will, there may be other difficulties, but this kind of discord and struggle will disappear.

SRI AUROBINDO

You aspire for a change, perhaps for a specific change; but the answer to your aspiration will not come immediately and in the meantime your nature will resist. Things happen like this: at a given moment the nature seems to have yielded and you think you have got the desired result. Your aspiration diminishes in intensity because you think you have the desired result. But the other fellow, who is very cunning and is waiting quietly in his corner, when you are off your guard, he springs up like a jack-in-the-box, and then you must begin all over again.

> *But if one can tear out completely the root of the thing?*

Ah! one must not be so sure of that. I have known people who wanted to save the world by reducing it so much that there was no longer a world left! This is the ascetic way – you want to do away with the problem by doing away with the possibility of the problem. But this will never change anything.

No, there is a method – a sure one – but your method must be very clear-sighted and you must have a wide-awake consciousness of your person and of what goes on there and the way in which things happen. Let us take the instance of a person subject to outbursts of rage and violence. According to one method he would be told: "Get as angry as you like, you will suffer the consequences of your anger and this will cure you." This could be discussed. According to another method he would be told: "Sit upon your anger and it will disappear." This too could be discussed. In any case, you will have to sit upon it all the time, for if ever you should get up for a minute you will see immediately what happens! Then, what is to be done?

You must become more and more conscious. You must observe how the thing happens, by what road the danger approaches, and stand in the way before it can take hold of you. If you want to cure yourself of a defect or a difficulty, there is but one method: to be perfectly vigilant, to have a very alert and vigilant consciousness. First you must see very clearly what you want to do. You must not hesitate, be full of doubt and say, "Is it good to do this or not, does this come into the synthesis or should it not come in?" You will see that if you trust your mind, it will always shuttle back and forth: it vacillates all the time. If you take a decision it will put before you all the arguments to show you that your decision is not good, and you will be tossed between the "yes" and "no", the black and white, and will arrive at nothing. Hence, first, you must know exactly what you want – know, not mentally, but through concentration, through aspiration and a very conscious will. That is the important point. Afterwards, gradually, by observation, by a sustained vigilance, you must realise a sort of method which will be personal to you – it is useless to convince others to adopt the same method as yours, for that won't succeed. Everyone must find his own method, everyone must have his own method, and to the

extent you put into practice your method, it will become
clearer and clearer, more and more precise. You can
correct a certain point, make clear another, etc. So, you
start working.... For a while, all will go well. Then, one
day, you will find yourself facing an insurmountable
difficulty and will tell yourself, "I have done all that and
here is everything as bad as before!" Then, in this case,
you must, through a yet more sustained concentration,
open an inner door in you and bring into this movement a
force which was not there formerly, a state of consciousness which was not there before. And there, there will be
a power, when your own personal power will be exhausted
and no longer effective. When the personal power runs
out ordinary people say, "That's good, I can no longer do
anything, it is finished." But I tell you that when you find
yourself before this wall, it is the beginning of something
new. By an obstinate concentration, you must pass over to
the other side of the wall and there you will find a new
knowledge, a new force, a new power, a new help, and
you will be able to work out a new system, a new method
which surely will take you very far.

THE MOTHER

The nature of your difficulty indicates the nature of the
victory you will gain, the victory you will exemplify in
Yoga. Thus, if there is persistent selfishness, it points to a
realisation of universality as your most prominent achievement in the future. And, when selfishness is there, you
have also the power to reverse this very difficulty into its
opposite, a victory of utter wideness.

When you have something to realise, you will have in

you just the characteristic which is the contradiction of that something. Face to face with the defect, the difficulty, you say, "Oh, I am like that! How awful it is!" But you ought to see the truth of the situation. Say to yourself, "My difficulty shows me clearly what I have ultimately to represent. To reach the absolute negation of it, the quality at the other pole – this is my mission."

Even in ordinary life, we have sometimes the experience of contraries. He who is very timid and has no courage in front of circumstances proves capable of bearing the most!

To one who has the aspiration for the Divine, the difficulty which is always before him is the door by which he will attain God in his own individual manner: it is his particular path towards the Divine Realisation.

There is also the fact that if somebody has a hundred difficulties it means he will have a tremendous realisation – provided, of course, there are in him patience and endurance and he keeps the aspiring flame of Agni burning against those defects.

And remember: the Grace of the Divine is generally proportioned to your difficulties.

THE MOTHER

You have said: "Everyone possesses... two opposite tendencies of character,... which are like the light and the shadow of the same thing." *

* "... everyone possesses in a large measure, and the exceptional individual in an increasing degree of precision, two opposite tendencies of character, in almost equal proportions, which are like the light and the shadow of the same thing. Thus someone who has the capacity of being

Why are things made in this way? Can't one have only the light?

Yes, if one eliminates the shadow. But it must be eliminated. That does not happen by itself. The world as it is is a mixed world. You cannot have an object which gets the light from one side without its casting a shadow on the other. It is like that, and indeed it is the shadows which make you see the lights. The world is like that, and to have only the light one must definitely go through the entire discipline necessary for eliminating the shadow. This is what I have explained a little farther; I have said that this shadow was like a sign of what you had to conquer in your nature in order to be able to realise what you have come to do. If you have a part to play, a mission to fulfil, you will always carry in yourself the main difficulty preventing you from realising it, so that you have within your reach the victory you must win. If you had to fight against a difficulty which is everywhere on earth, it would be very difficult (you would need to have a very vast consciousness and a very great power), while if you carry in your own nature just the shadow or defect you must conquer, well, it is there, within your reach: you

-----

exceptionally generous will suddenly find an obstinate avarice rising up in his nature, the courageous man will be a coward in some part of his being and the good man will suddenly have wicked impulses. In this way life seems to endow everyone not only with the possibility of expressing an ideal, but also with contrary elements representing in a concrete manner the battle he has to wage and the victory he has to win for the realisation to become possible." (The Mother, *On Education*, CWM, Vol. 12, p. 19.)

see all the time the effects of this thing and can fight it directly, immediately. It is a very practical organisation.

THE MOTHER

The whole purpose of the Yoga is to gather all the divergent parts together and forge them into an undivided unity. Till then you cannot hope to be without difficulties – difficulties, for example, like doubt or depression or hesitation. The whole world is full of the poison. You take it in with every breath. If you exchange a few words with an undesirable man or even if such a man merely passes by you, you may catch the contagion from him. It is sufficient for you to come near a place where there is plague in order to be infected with its poison; you need not know at all that it is there. You can lose in a few minutes what it has taken you months to gain. So long as you belong to humanity and so long as you lead the ordinary life, it does not matter much if you mix with the people of the world; but if you want the divine life, you will have to be exceedingly careful about your company and your environment.

THE MOTHER

Naturally, the more one-pointed the aspiration the swifter the progress. The difficulty comes when either the vital with its desires or the physical with its past habitual movements comes in – as they do with almost everyone. It is then that the dryness and difficulty of spontaneous aspiration come. This dryness is a well-known obstacle in all sadhana. But one has to persist and not be discouraged.

If one keeps the will fixed even in these barren periods, they pass and after their passage a greater force of aspiration and experience becomes possible.

SRI AUROBINDO

The up and down movement which you speak of is common to all ways of yoga. It is there in the path of bhakti, but there are equally alternations of states of light and states of darkness, sometimes sheer and prolonged darkness, when one follows the path of knowledge. Those who have occult experiences come to periods when all experiences cease and even seem finished for ever. Even when there have been many and permanent realisations, these seem to go behind the veil and leave nothing in front except a dull blank, filled, if at all, only with recurrent attacks and difficulties. These alternations are the result of the nature of human consciousness and are not a proof of unfitness or of predestined failure. One has to be prepared for them and pass through. They are the "day and night" of the Vedic mystics.

SRI AUROBINDO

Everyone has these alternations because the total consciousness is not able to remain always in the above experience. The point is that in the intervals there should be quietude, at least in the inner being, no restlessness, dissatisfaction or struggle. If that point is attained, then the sadhana can go on smoothly – not that there will be no difficulties but there will be no disquietude or dissatisfaction etc. etc.

SRI AUROBINDO

The reason why there are these alternations of which you complain is that the nature of the consciousness is like that; after a little spell of wakefulness it feels the need of a little sleep. Very often in the beginning the wakings are brief, the sleeps long; afterwards it becomes more equal and later on the sleep periods are shorter and shorter. Another cause of these alternations, when one is receiving, is the nature's need of closing up to assimilate. It can take perhaps a great deal, but while the experience is going on it cannot absorb properly what it brings, so it closes down for assimilation. A third cause comes in the period of transformation, – one part of the nature changes and one feels for a time as if there had been a complete and permanent change. But one is disappointed to find it cease and a period of barrenness or lowered consciousness follow. This is because another part of the consciousness comes up for change and a period of preparation and veiled working follows which seems to be one of unenlightenment or worse. These things alarm, disappoint or perplex the eagerness and impatience of the sadhak; but if one takes them quietly and knows how to use them or adopt the right attitude, one can make these unenlightened periods also a part of the conscious sadhana.

SRI AUROBINDO

The real reason of the difficulty and the constant alternation is the struggle between the veiled true being within and the outer nature, especially the lower vital full of desires and the physical mind full of obscurity and ignorance. The struggle is inevitable in human nature and no sadhak escapes it; everyone has to deal with that obscurity and resistance and its obstinacy and constant recurrence; for the lower nature is not only persistent in its repetitions and returns, but even when it is on the point of changing, the general Powers of that plane in universal Nature try to keep up the resistance by bringing back the old movements at each step in order to prevent the progress from being confirmed for good and made final. It is true therefore that a constant sadhana persistent and unceasing is necessary if one wants to go quickly – though even otherwise one will arrive if the soul within has the call, for the soul will persist and after each obscuration or stumble will bring back the light and drive one on on the path till it feels that it is at last secure of a smooth and easy march to the goal.

Sri Aurobindo

Even before the tranquillising purification of the outer nature has been effected or before it is sufficient, one can still break down the wall screening our inner being from our outer awareness by a strong force of call and aspiration, a vehement will or violent effort or an effective discipline or process; but this may be a premature movement and is not without its serious dangers. In entering within one may find oneself amidst a chaos of unfamiliar and supernormal experiences to which one has not the key or a press of subliminal or cosmic forces, subconscient, mental, vital, subtle-physical, which may unduly sway or chaotically drive the being, encircle it in a cave of darkness, or keep it wandering in a wilderness of glamour, allurement, deception, or push it into an obscure battlefield full of secret and treacherous and misleading or open and violent oppositions; beings and voices and influences may appear to the inner sense and vision and hearing claiming to be the Divine Being or His messengers or Powers and Godheads of the Light or guides of the path to realisation, while in truth they are of a very different character. If there is too much egoism in the nature of the seeker or a strong passion or an excessive ambition, vanity or other dominating weakness, or an obscurity of the mind or a vacillating will or a weakness of the life-force or an unsteadiness in it or want of balance, he is likely to be seized on through these deficiencies and to be frustrated or to deviate, misled from the true way of the inner life and seeking into false paths, or to be left wandering about in an intermediate chaos of experiences and fail to find his way out into the true realisation. These perils were well-known to a past spiritual experience and have been met by imposing the necessity of initiation, of discipline, of methods of purification and testing by ordeal, of an entire submission to the directions of the path-finder or path-leader, one who has realised the Truth and himself possesses and is able to communicate the light, the experience, a guide who is strong to take by the hand and carry over difficult passages as well as to instruct and point out the way. But even so the dangers will be there and can only be surmounted if there is or there grows up a complete sincerity, a will for purity, a readiness for obedience to the Truth, for surrender to the Highest, a readiness to lose or to subject to a divine yoke the limiting and self-affirming ego. These things are the sign that the true will for realisation, for conversion of the conscious-ness, for transformation is there, the necessary stage of the evolution has been reached: in that condition the defects of nature which belong to the human being cannot be a permanent obstacle to the change from the mental to the spiritual status; the process may never be entirely easy, but the way will have been made open and practicable.

SRI AUROBINDO

Everything once gained is there and can be regained. Yoga is not a thing that goes by one decisive rush one way or the other – it is a building up of a new consciousness and is full of ups and downs. But if one keeps to it the ups have a habit of resulting by accumulation in a decisive change – therefore the one thing to do is to keep at it. After a fall don't wail and say, "I'm done for," but get up, dust yourself and proceed farther on the right path.

SRI AUROBINDO

VII

GROWTH OF CONSCIOUSNESS
INNER EXPERIENCES

There are two classes of things that happen in yoga, realisations and experiences. Realisations are the reception in the consciousness and the establishment there of the fundamental truths of the Divine, of the Higher or Divine Nature, of the world-consciousness and the play of its forces, of one's own self and real nature and the inner nature of things, the power of these things growing in one till they are a part of one's inner life and existence, – as for instance, the realisation of the Divine Presence, the descent and settling of the higher Peace, Light, Force, Ananda in the consciousness, their workings there, the realisation of the divine or spiritual love, the perception of one's own psychic being, the discovery of one's own true mental being, true vital being, true physical being, the realisation of the overmind or the supramental consciousness, the clear perception of the relation of all these things to our present inferior nature and their action on it to change that lower nature. The list, of course, might be infinitely longer. These things also are often called experiences when they only come in flashes, snatches or rare visitations; they are spoken of as full realisations only when they become very positive or frequent or continuous or normal.

SRI AUROBINDO

Experiences and descents are very good for preparation, but change of consciousness is the thing wanted – it is the proof that the experiences and descents have had an effect.

SRI AUROBINDO

GROWTH OF CONSCIOUSNESS
INNER EXPERIENCES

On what do experiences depend, Mother?

Ah, it depends on many things.... Some people have
experiences quite spontaneously and it is understood that
this depends on their former lives or the way in which they
were formed, the forces which presided over the construction of their present physical being, and the influence
they came under even before their birth. These people
have experiences spontaneously. There are not many of
these, but there are some. There are others for whom it is
the result of a very sustained effort. They aspire to have
experiences and impose a discipline upon themselves or
adopt a discipline so as to be able to have them. Sometimes it takes very long to obtain something. It depends
altogether upon the way one is built. I knew people who
were ignorant, yes, and who had quite remarkable experiences of clairvoyance, of inner perception. They understood nothing of what was happening to them or of what
they saw. But they had the gift.

But then this has no effect on their outer life, has it?

No.

Then what's the use of having experiences?

It is not a question of "use". Not everything in the world is
utilitarian. It's like that because it's like that. Yes, you can
say "what's the use" to someone who is exclusively

preoccupied with having experiences, who has no inner intellectual and spiritual preparation, and who through some sort of fantasy would like to have experiences. You could say to him, "Yes, what's the use? It is not this that will lead you to the spiritual life. It can help you if you have taken up the path. And if you have taken up the path in all sincerity, well, they will come to the extent that they are useful. But to seek experience for experience's sake is altogether useless." And you can tell people, "What's the good? It is a fantasy, a fantasy on another plane; it is another kind of desire, but it is a desire."

However, in the normal course, to the degree that you progress inwardly, every step that you take towards the true consciousness is accompanied by a certain number of experiences corresponding to it which allow you to understand the situation you are in: this of course is normal. It ought to be like that.

But these usually are not such sensational experiences as to be made much of. People often have all of a sudden an illumination of consciousness, an inner indication, an unusual perception. But when they are not turned exclusively towards the desire to have experiences, they don't attach much importance to it. Sometimes they don't even attach enough importance. The indication came, showed them something, but they were not even aware of it. Yet it is not these things which give you the impression that you are living in a wonderful world. These things are quite normal. Suddenly an opening in the mind, a light that comes, one understands something which he did not before. You take that for a very natural phenomenon. But it is a spiritual experience – or the clear seeing of a situation, the understanding of what is happening in oneself, of the state one is in, the indication of the exact progress one ought to make, of the thing that's to be corrected. This too is an experience and an experience that comes from within; it is indication given to you by the psychic. People take this also as quite a natural fact. They do not attach any importance to it.

Usually people mean by "experience" either altogether extravagant phenomena, levitation and things like that, or else sensational visions: being able to see the future or seeing at a distance or maybe ordinary things like being able to tell where a lost object can be found or all kinds of little tricks like that. This is what people call "experiences".

Well, usually people who have these faculties are not well educated, but for some reason they are born with a gift, as some are born musicians, others painters, and others scientists. These are born clairvoyants, and so it may be, when they are in need they use this faculty to earn their living, and they spoil it completely. If they happen to be in comfortable circumstances and do not need to earn their living, then they become famous among their friends. In any case, this is always an opportunity for a certain kind of commercialism. There are very few who can have these gifts without using them either to make a name for themselves or to earn money. But these gifts are not of a very high level. One can have them without having a very spiritual life. They do not depend at all on an inner spiritual height. One should not mistake them for signs of progress.

Besides, one thing is certain: those who do not have these faculties and want to acquire them, for instance the capacity of foresight, foreseeing what is going to come, which is analogous to prophecy, the capacity to know events before they happen – as I said, there are people who have this spontaneously because of some peculiarity from birth – and if one wants to acquire them himself, that is to say, enter into contact with regions where these things can be seen – and not by chance or accidentally or without having any control over the thing, but on the contrary to see them at will – then this indeed means a *formidable* work. And that is why some people attach a very great value to these things. But they have some value only when they are under one's control, done at will and the result of an inner discipline. In this case, yes, because this proves that you have entered into contact with a certain region where it is difficult to enter consciously, at will, and permanently. It is very difficult, it requires much development. And then, for you to be sure of what you have seen... because I haven't told you that with these people who make a profession of their clairvoyance, it becomes... I said "commercialism", but it is worse than that, you know, it is a fraud! When they do not see anything, they invent. When they make a profession of it, and people come to ask them something about the future, and they can see nothing at all, they are obliged to invent something, otherwise they would lose their reputation and their clientele. So this becomes a deception, you see, a falsehood, fraud or falsification.

But when one wants to have a pure, correct information, to be in contact with the truth of things, and see in advance – not according to one's petty mental construction, but how things are decreed, in the place where they are decreed and the time when they are decreed – then that requires a *very great* mental purity, a *very great* vital equilibrium, an absence of desire, of preference. One must never want anything to be of one kind or another, for this falsifies your vision immediately.

All who have visions usually deform them, *all*, almost *without exception*. I don't think there is one in a million who doesn't deform his vision, because the minute it touches the brain it touches the domain of preferences, desires, attachments, and this indeed is enough to give a colouring, a special look to what you have seen. Even if you have seen correctly, you translate it wrongly in your consciousness. This truly asks for a great perfection. But you can have perfection without the gift of vision. And the perfection can be as great without the gift as with it. If it interests you specially, you can make an effort to obtain it. But only if it interests you specially. If you lay great store by knowing certain things, you can undertake a discipline; you may undertake a discipline also in order to change the functioning of your senses. I think I have already explained to you how one can hear at a distance, see at a distance, even physically; but this means considerable effort, which perhaps is not always in proportion to the result, because these are side issues, not the central, the most important thing. These are side issues which may be interesting, but in itself this is not the spiritual life; one may have a spiritual life wihtout this. Now, the two together can give you perhaps a greater capacity. But for this too you must tell yourself, "If I ought to have it – if I take the true attitude of surrender to the Divine and of complete consecration – if I ought to have it I shall have it. As, if I ought to have the gift of speech, I shall have it." And in fact, if one is truly surrendered, in the true way and totally, at every minute one is what he ought to be and does what he ought to do and knows what he ought to know. This... but naturally, for this one should have overcome the petty limitations of the ego, and this does not happen overnight. But it can happen.

THE MOTHER

... you speak of your experiences as vague and dream-like. In the first place the scorn of small experiences in the inner life is no part of wisdom, reason or common sense. It is in the beginning of the sadhana and for a long time, the small experiences that come on each other and, if given their full value, prepare the field, build up a preparatory consciousness and one day break open the walls to big experiences. But if you despise them with the ambitious idea that you must have either the big experiences or nothing, it is not surprising that they come once in a blue moon and cannot do their work. Moreover, all your experiences were not small. There were some like the stilling descent of a Power in the body – what you used to call numbness – which anyone with spiritual knowledge would have recognised as a first strong step towards the opening of the consciousness to the higher Peace and Light. But it was not in the line of your expectations and you gave it no special value. As for vague and dream-like, you feel it so because you are looking at them and at everything that happens in you from the standpoint of the outward physical mind and intellect which can take only physical things as real and important and vivid and to it inward phenomena are something unreal, vague and truthless. The spiritual experience does not even despise dreams and visions; it is known to it that many of these things are not dreams at all but experiences on an inner

plane and if the experiences of the inner planes which lead
to the opening of the inner self into the outer so as to
influence and change it are not accepted, the experiences
of the subtle consciousness and the trance consciousness,
how is the waking consciousness to expand out of the
narrow prison of the body and body-mind and the senses?
For, to the physical mind untouched by the inner
awakened consciousness, even the experience of the
cosmic consciousness or the Eternal Self might very well
seem merely subjective and unconvincing. It would think,
"Curious, no doubt, rather interesting, but very subjective, don't you think? Hallucinations, yes!" The first
business of the spiritual seeker is to get away from the
outward mind's outlook and to look at inward phenomena
with an inward mind to which they soon become powerful
and stimulating realities. If one does that, then one begins
to see that there is here a wide field of truth and
knowledge, in which one can move from discovery to
discovery to reach the supreme discovery of all.

SRI AUROBINDO

There is no law that a feeling cannot be an experience;
experiences are of all kinds and take all forms in the
consciousness. When the consciousness undergoes, sees
or feels anything spiritual or psychic or even occult, that is
an experience – in the technical yogic sense, for there are
of course all sorts of experiences that are not of that
character. The feelings themselves are of many kinds. The
word feeling is often used for an emotion, and there can
be psychic or spiritual emotions which are numbered
among yogic experiences, such as a wave of *śuddhā bhakti*

or the rising of love towards the Divine. A feeling also means a perception of something felt – a perception in the vital or psychic or in the essential substance of the consciousness. I find even often a mental perception when it is very vivid described as a feeling. If you exclude all these feelings and kindred ones and say that they are feelings, not experiences, then there is very little room left for experiences at all. Feeling and vision are the main forms of spiritual experience. One sees and feels the Brahman everywhere; one feels a force enter or go out from one; one feels or sees the presence of the Divine within or around one; one feels or sees the descent of Light; one feels the descent of Peace or Ananda. Kick out all that on the ground that it is only a feeling and you make a clean sweep of most of the things that we call experience. Again, we feel a change in the substance of the consciousness or the state of consciousness. We feel ourselves spreading in wideness and the body as a small thing in the wideness (this can be seen also); we feel the heart-consciousness being wide instead of narrow, soft instead of hard, illumined instead of obscure, the head-consciousness also, the vital, even the physical; we feel thousands of things of all kinds and why are we not to call them experience? Of course it is an inner sight, an inner feeling, subtle feeling, not material, like the feeling of a cold wind or a stone or any other object, but as the inner consciousness deepens it is not less vivid or concrete, it is even more so.

SRI AUROBINDO

Experiences come to many before the nature is ready to

make full profit from them; to others a more or less prolonged period of purification and preparation of the stuff of the nature or the instruments comes first, while experiences are held up till this process is largely or wholly over. The latter method is the safer and sounder of the two.

SRI AUROBINDO

You did quite right in first developing the sattwic qualities and building up the inner meditative quietude. It is possible by strenuous meditation or by certain methods of tense endeavour to open doors on to the inner being or even break down some of the walls between the inner and outer self before finishing or even undertaking this preliminary self-discipline, but it is not always wise to do it as that may lead to conditions of sadhana which may be very turbid, chaotic, beset with unnecessary dangers. By adopting the more patient course you have arrived at a point at which the doors of the inner being have begun almost automatically to swing open. Now both processes can go on side by side, but it is necessary to keep the sattwic quietude, patience, vigilance, – to hurry nothing, to force nothing, not to be led away by any strong lure or call of the intermediate stage which is now beginning, before you are sure that it is the right call. For there are many vehement pulls from the forces of the inner planes which it is not safe to follow.

SRI AUROBINDO

The intermediate zone means simply a confused condition

or passage in which one is getting out of the personal consciousness and opening into the cosmic (cosmic Mind, cosmic vital, cosmic physical, something perhaps of the cosmic higher Mind) without having yet transcended the human mind levels. One is not in possession of or direct contact with the divine Truth *on its own levels*, but one can receive something from them, even from the overmind, indirectly. Only, as one is still immersed in the cosmic Ignorance, all that comes from above can be mixed, perverted, taken hold of for their purposes by lower, even by hostile Powers.

It is not necessary for everyone to struggle through the intermediate zone. If one has purified oneself, if there is no abnormal vanity, egoism, ambition or other strong misleading element, or if one is vigilant and on one's guard, or if the psychic is in front, one can either pass rapidly and directly or with a minimum of trouble into the higher zones of consciousness where one is in direct contact with the Divine Truth.

SRI AUROBINDO

I mean by it [the intermediate zone] that when the sadhak gets beyond the barriers of his own embodied personal mind he enters into a wide range of experiences which are not the limited solid physical truth of things and not yet either the spiritual truth of things. It is a zone of formations, mental, vital, subtle physical, and whatever one forms or is formed by the forces of these worlds in us becomes for the sadhak for a time the truth – unless he is guided and listens to his guide. Afterwards if he gets through he discovers what it was and passes on into the subtle truth of things. It is a borderland where all the worlds meet, mental, vital, subtle physical, pseudo-spiritual – but there is no order or firm foothold – a passage between the physical and the true spiritual realms.

SRI AUROBINDO

Anyone passing the border of ordinary consciousness can enter into this [intermediate] zone, if he does not take care to enter into the psychic. In itself there is no harm in passing through, provided one does not stop there. But ego, sex, ambition, etc., if they get exaggerated, can easily lead to a dangerous downfall.

SRI AUROBINDO

It [the breaking of the veil] comes of itself with the pressure of the sadhana. It can also be brought about by specific concentration and effort.

It is certainly better if the psychic is conscious and active before there is the removing of the veil or screen between the individual and the universal consciousness which comes when the inner being is brought forward in all its wideness. For then there is much less danger of the difficulties of what I have called the Intermediate Zone.

SRI AUROBINDO

I do not question at all the personal intensity or concreteness of your internal experiences, but experiences can be intense and yet be very mixed in their truth and their character. In your experience your own subjectivity, sometimes your ego-pushes interfere very much and give them their form and the impression they create on you. It is only if there is a pure psychic response that the form given to the experience is likely to be the right one and the mental and vital movements will then present themselves in their true nature. Otherwise the mind, the vital, the ego give their own colour to what happens, their own turn, very usually their own deformation. *Intensity* is not a guarantee of entire truth and correctness in an experience; it is only *purity* of the consciousness that can give an entire truth and correctness.

SRI AUROBINDO

Merely to have experiences of the higher consciousness will not change the nature. Either the higher consciousness has to make a dynamic descent into the whole being and change it; or it must establish itself in the inner being down to the inner physical so that the latter feels itself separate from the outer and is able to act freely upon it; or the psychic must come forward and change the nature; or the inner will must awake and force the nature to change. These are the four ways in which change can be brought about.

SRI AUROBINDO

To change the nature is not easy and always takes time, but if there is no inner experience, no gradual emergence of the other purer consciousness that is concealed by all these things you now see, it would be almost impossible even for the strongest will. You say that first you must get rid of all these things, then have the inner experiences. But how is that to be done? These things, anger, jealousy, desire are the very stuff of the ordinary human vital consciousness. They could not be changed if there were not a deeper consciousness within which is of quite another character. There is within you a psychic being which is divine, directly a part of the Mother, pure of all these defects. It is covered and concealed by the ordinary consciousness and nature, but when it is unveiled and able to come forward and govern the being, then it changes the ordinary consciousness, throws all these undivine things out and changes the outer nature altogether. That is why we want the sadhaks to concentrate, to open this concealed consciousness – it is by concentration of whatever kind and the experiences it brings that one opens and becomes aware within and the new consciousness and nature begin to grow and come out. Of course we want them also to use their will and reject the desires and wrong movements of the vital, for by doing that the emergence of the true consciousness becomes possible. But rejection alone cannot succeed; it is by rejection and by inner experience and growth that it is done.

SRI AUROBINDO

... there are three rules of the sadhana which are very necessary in an earlier stage and which you should remember. First, open yourself to experience but do not take the *bhoga* of the experiences. Do not attach yourself to any particular kind of experience. Do not take all ideas and suggestions as true and do not take any knowledge, voice or thought-message as absolutely final and definitive.

SRI AUROBINDO

These voices are sometimes one's own mental formations, sometimes suggestions from outside. Good or bad depends on what they say and on the quarter from which they come.

SRI AUROBINDO

Anybody can get "voices" – there are first the movements of one's nature that take upon themselves a voice – then there are all sorts of beings who either for a joke or for a serious purpose invade with their voices.

SRI AUROBINDO

Lights are of all kinds, supramental, mental, vital, physical, divine or Asuric – one has to watch, grow in experience and learn to know one from another. The true lights however are by their clarity and beauty not difficult to recognise.

The current from above and the current from below are familiar features of yogic experience. It is the energy of the higher Nature and the energy of the lower Nature that become active and turned towards each other and move to meet, one descending, the other ascending. What happens when they meet depends on the sadhak. If his constant will is for the purification of the lower by the higher consciousness, then the meeting results in that and in spiritual progress. If his mind and vital are turbid and clouded, there is a clash, an impure mixture and much disturbance.

SRI AUROBINDO

The experience you relate, the stillness, the emptiness of mind and vital and cessation of thoughts and other movements was the coming of the state called "samadhi" in which the consciousness goes inside in a deep stillness and silence. This condition is favourable to inner experience, realisation, the vision of the unseen truth of things, though one can get these in the waking condition also. It is not sleep but the state in which one feels conscious within, no longer outside.

SRI AUROBINDO

The usual rule given by yogis is that one should not speak of one's experience to others except of course the Guru while the sadhana is going on because it wastes the experience, there is what they call *kṣaya* of the tapasya. It is only long past experiences that they speak of and even that not too freely.

SRI AUROBINDO

The Light left you because you spoke of it to someone who was not an *adhikārī*. It is safest not to speak of these experiences except to a Guru or to one who can help you. The passing away of an experience as soon as it is spoken of is a frequent happening and for that reason many yogis make it a rule never to speak of what happens within them, unless it is a thing of the past or a settled realisation that nothing can take away.

SRI AUROBINDO

For most people an experience exists only when they can explain it to themselves. The experience in itself – contact with a certain force, a widening of consciousness, communion with an aspect of the Divine, no matter what experience, an opening of the being, the breaking down of an obstacle, crossing over a stage, opening new doors – all these experiences, if people cannot explain them to themselves in so many words and materialise them in precise thoughts, it is as though these did not exist! And it is just this need for expression, this need for translation, which causes the greater part of the experience to lose its power of action on the individual consciousness. How is it that you have a decisive, definitive experience, that, for instance, you have opened the door of your psychic being, you have been in communion with it, you know what this means, and then – it does not stay? It is because it does not have a sufficiently tangible power unless you can express it to yourself. The experience begins for you only when you are able to describe it. Well, when you are able to describe it, the greater part of its intensity and its capacity of action for the inner and outer transformation has already evaporated. There it may be said that expression, explanation is always a coming down. The experience itself is on a much higher plane.

THE MOTHER

"One must always be greater than one's experience."

Whatever may be the nature, the strength and wonder of an experience, you must not be dominated by it to such an extent that it governs your entire being and you lose your balance and your contact with a reasonable and calm attitude. That is to say, when you enter in some way into contact with a force or consciousness which surpasses yours, instead of being entirely dominated by this consciousness or force, you must always be able to remind yourself that it is only *one* experience among thousands and thousands of others, and that, consequently, its nature is not absolute, it is relative. No matter how beautiful it may be, you can and ought to have better ones: however exceptional it may be, there are others still more marvellous; and however high it may be, you can always rise still higher in future. So, instead of losing one's head one places the experience in the chain of development and keeps a healthy physical balance so as not to lose the sense of relativity with ordinary life. In this way, there is no risk.

The means?... One who knows how to do this will always find it very easy, but for one who doesn't know it is perhaps a little... a little troublesome.

There is a means.

It is never to lose the idea of the total self-giving to the Grace which is the expression of the Supreme. When one gives oneself, when one surrenders, entrusts oneself entirely to That which is above, beyond all creation, and when, instead of seeking any personal advantage from the experience, one makes an offering of it to the divine Grace and knows that it is from This that the experience comes and that it is to This that the result of the experience must be given back, then one is quite safe.

In other words: no ambition, no vanity, no pride. A sincere self-giving, a sincere humility, and one is sheltered from all danger. There you are, this is what I call being greater than one's experience.

THE MOTHER

Mother, why is it that the same contemplation does not always produce the same sensation in oneself? That is, for example, when one looks at the sea or the stars and thinks of one's insignificance, then there is a particular sensation which is produced within, and then at another time, when one wants to have the same experience, even if one thinks about it, why doesn't it recur?

One can never have the same experience twice because one is never the same person twice. Between the first experience and the second, even if one hour has passed, you are no longer the same man and you can never reproduce identically the same thing. If you take care to become more conscious, more sincere, more concentrated, the experience you have will be different, but it may be deeper and more clear. But if you cling to something you have had and want to reproduce the same thing, you will have nothing at all, because you can't have the same thing and you are in a state in which you refuse to have a new experience, for you are attached to the past one. And usually when one has had an experience which was a revelation, something altogether important, one doesn't want to leave it, one is afraid of not having it any longer, and so, in this movement of clinging on to something, one prevents oneself from progressing and puts oneself in conditions in which one can't have the next experience.

Well, this has to be understood, because it is an absolute fact: one can never have the same experience twice. There may be similar experiences, very close, and particularly some which appear similar, but these experiences... if one is absolutely sincere, impartial and like a blank page, he will perceive that there is a difference, sometimes an essential one, between the two, though in appearance they seem very close. But the more ready you are to leave behind all that you have experienced, in order to be able to go towards something better and higher, the faster you will go; the more you drag the heavy weight of all the past which you don't want to get rid of, the slower is your advance.

All the past should always be simply like a stepping-stone or a ladder, something to lead you farther; it should not have any other use except to push you forward. And if you can feel this and always turn your back on what is past and look at what you want to do, then you go much faster, you don't waste time on the way. What makes you lose time is always this clinging to what has been, to what is, what seemed to you beautiful and good in what is past. This must only help you, you must not reject it, but it must help you to go forward, it must simply be something on which you lean to take a step forward.

Now, at a particular time, a set of circumstances, inner and outer, has caused one to be receptive to a certain vibration; for example, as you say, while looking at the stars or contemplating a landscape or reading a page or hearing a lecture, one has suddenly an inner revelation, an experience, something that strikes him and gives him the impression of being open to something new. But if you want to hold on to this tightly like that, you will lose everything, because one can't keep the past, one must always go forward, advance, advance. This illumination must prepare you so that you can organise your whole being on this new level, in order to be able suddenly, one day, to leap up again to a higher step.

There is a horizontal advance between abrupt ascents. It is the moment of the abrupt ascent which gives you an impression of something like a revelation, a great inner joy. But once you have climbed the step, if you want to climb it once more you would have to go down again. You must go on preparing yourself at this level in order to climb another higher step. These things which suddenly give you a great joy are always ascents. But these ascents are prepared by a slow work of horizontal progress, that is, one must become more and more conscious, establish more and more perfectly what one is, draw from it all the inner, psychological consequences, and in action also. It is a long utilisation of an abrupt leap and, as I say, there are two kinds of progress. But the horizontal progress is indispensable.

You must not stop, you must not cling in this way to your vertical progress and not want to move because it has brought you a revelation. You must know how to leave it in order to prepare for another.

THE MOTHER

VIII

THE PSYCHIC BEING AND INNER GROWTH

It is the soul in us which turns always towards Truth, Good and Beauty, because it is by these things that it itself grows in stature; the rest, their opposites, are a necessary part of experience, but have to be outgrown in the spiritual increase of the being. The fundamental psychic entity in us has the delight of life and all experience as part of the progressive manifestation of the spirit, but the very principle of its delight of life is to gather out of all contacts and happenings their secret divine sense and essence, a divine use and purpose so that by experience our mind and life may grow out of the Inconscience towards a supreme consciousness, out of the divisions of the Ignorance towards an integralising consciousness and knowledge. It is there for that and it pursues from life to life its ever-increasing upward tendency and insistence; the growth of the soul is a growth out of darkness into light, out of falsehood into truth, out of suffering into its own supreme and universal Ananda.

SRI AUROBINDO

There are, we might say, two beings in us, one on the surface, our ordinary exterior mind, life, body consciousness, another behind the veil, an inner mind, an inner life, an inner physical consciousness constituting another or inner self. This inner self once awake opens in its turn to our true real eternal self. It opens inwardly to the soul, called in the language of this yoga the psychic being which supports our successive births and at each birth assumes a new mind, life and body. It opens above to the Self or Spirit which is unborn and by conscious recovery of it we transcend the changing personality and achieve freedom and full mastery over our nature.

SRI AUROBINDO

THE PSYCHIC BEING AND INNER GROWTH

It is necessary to understand clearly the difference between the evolving soul (psychic being) and the pure
Atman, self or spirit. The pure self is unborn, does not
pass through death or birth, is independent of birth or
body, mind or life or this manifested Nature. It is not
bound by these things, not limited, not affected, even
though it assumes and supports them. The soul, on the
contrary, is something that comes down into birth and
passes through death – although it does not itself die, for it
is immortal – from one state to another, from the earth
plane to other planes and back again to the earth-existence.
It goes on with this progression from life to life through an
evolution which leads it up to the human state and evolves
through it all a being of itself which we call the psychic
being that supports the evolution and develops a physical,
a vital, a mental human consciousness as its instruments of
world-experience and of a disguised, imperfect, but
growing self-expression. All this it does from behind a veil
showing something of its divine self only in so far as the
imperfection of the instrumental being will allow it. But a
time comes when it is able to prepare to come out from
behind the veil, to take command and turn all the instrumental nature towards a divine fulfilment. This is the
beginning of the true spiritual life. The soul is able now to
make itself ready for a higher evolution of manifested
consciousness than the mental human – it can pass from
the mental to the spiritual and through degrees of the
spiritual to the supramental state. Till then there is no
reason why it should cease from birth, it cannot in fact do
so. If having reached the spiritual state, it wills to pass out

of the terrestrial manifestation, it may indeed do so – but there is also possible a higher manifestation, in the Knowledge and not in the Ignorance.

SRI AUROBINDO

The human individual is a very complex being: he is composed of innumerable elements, each one of which is an independent entity and has almost a personality. Not only so, the most contradictory elements are housed together. If there is a particular quality or capacity present, the very opposite of it, annulling it, as it were, will also be found along with it and embracing it. I have seen a man brave, courageous, heroic to the extreme, flinching from no danger, facing unperturbed the utmost peril, truly the bravest of the brave; and yet I have seen the same man cowering in abject terror, like the last of poltroons, in the presence of certain circumstances. I have seen a most generous man giving things away largely, freely, not counting any expenditure or sacrifice, without the least care or reservation; the same person I have also found to be the vilest of misers with respect to certain other considerations. Again, I have seen the most intelligent person, with a clear mind, full of light and understanding, easily comprehending the logic and implication of a topic; and yet I have seen him betraying the utmost stupidity of which even an ordinary man without education or intelligence would be incapable. These are not theoretical examples: I have come across such persons actually in life.

The complexity arises not only in extension but also in depth. Man does not live on a single plane but on many planes at the same time. There is a scale of gradation in human consciousness: the higher one rises in the scale the greater the number of elements or personalities that one possesses. Whether one lives mostly or mainly on the physical or vital or mental plane or on any particular section of these planes or on the planes above and beyond them, there will be, accordingly, differences in the consti-tution or psycho-physical make-up of the individual personality. The higher one stands, the richer the per-sonality, because it lives not only on its own normal level but also on all the levels that are below it and which it has transcended. The complete or integral man, some occul-tists say, possesses three hundred and sixty-five personal-ities; indeed it may be much more. The Vedas speak of the three and thirty-three and thirty-three hundred and thirty-three thousand gods that may be housed in the human vehicle — the basic three being evidently the triple status or world of Body, Life and Mind.

What is the meaning of this self-contradiction, this division in man? To understand that, we must know and remember that each person represents a certain quality or capacity, a particular achievement to be embodied. How best can it be done? What is the way by which one can acquire a quality at its purest, highest and most perfect? It is by setting an opposition to it. That is how a power is increased and strengthened – by fighting against and overcoming all that weakens and contradicts it. The deficiencies with respect to a particular quality show you where you have to mend and reinforce it and in what way to improve it in order to make it perfectly perfect. It is the hammer that beats the weak and soft iron to transform it into hard steel. The preliminary discord is useful and needs to be utilised for a higher harmony. This is the secret of self-conflict in man. You are weakest precisely in that element which is destined to be your greatest asset.

Each man has then a mission to fulfil, a role to play in the universe, a part he has been given to learn and take up in the cosmic Purpose, a part which he alone is capable of executing and none other. This he has to learn and acquire through life-experiences, that is to say, not in one life but in life after life. In fact, that is the meaning of the chain of lives that the individual has to pass through, namely, to acquire experiences and to gather from them the thread – the skein of qualities and attributes, powers and capacities – for the pattern of life he has to weave. Now, the inmost being, the true personality, the central consciousness of the evolving individual is his psychic being. It is, as it were, a very tiny spark of light lying in normal people far behind the life-experiences. In grown-up souls this psychic consciousness has an increased light – increased in intensity, volume and richness. Thus there are old souls and new souls. Old and ancient are those that have reached or are about to reach the fullness of perfection; they have passed through a long history of innumerable lives and developed the most complex and yet the most integrated personality. New souls are those that have just emerged or are now emerging out of the mere physico-vital existence; they are like simple organisms, made of fewer constituents related mostly to the bodily life, with just a modicum of the mental. It is the soul, however, that grows with experiences and it is the soul that builds and enriches the personality. Whatever portion of the outer life, whatever element in the mind or vital or body succeeds in coming into contact with the psychic consciousness – that is to say, is able to come under its influence – is taken up and lodged there: it remains in the psychic being as its living memory and permanent possession. It is such elements that form the basis, the groundwork upon which the structure of the integral and true personality is raised.

The first thing to do then is to find out what it is that you are meant to realise, what is the role you have to play, your particular mission, and the capacity or quality you have to express. You have to discover that and also the thing or things that oppose and do not allow it to flower or come to full manifestation. In other words, you have to know yourself, recognise your soul or psychic being.

For that you must be absolutely sincere and impartial. You must observe yourself as if you were observing and criticising a third person. You must not start with an idea that this is your life's mission, this is your particular capacity, this you are to do or that you are to do, in this lies your talent or genius, etc. That will carry you away from the right track. It is not the liking or disliking of your external being, your mental or vital or physical choice that determines the true line of your growth. Nor should you take up the opposite attitude and say, "I am good for nothing in this matter, I am useless in that one; it is not for me." Neither vanity and arrogance nor self-depreciation and false modesty should move you. As I said, you must be absolutely impartial and unconcerned. You should be like a mirror that reflects the truth and does not judge.

If you are able to keep such an attitude, if you have this repose and quiet trust in your being and wait for what may be revealed to you, then something like this happens: you are, as it were, in a wood, dark and noiseless; you see in front of you merely a sheet of water, dark and still, hardly visible – a bit of a pond imbedded in the obscurity; and slowly upon it a moonbeam is cast and in the cool dim light emerges the calm liquid surface. That is how your secret truth of being will appear and present itself to you at your first contact with it: there you will see gradually reflected the true qualities of your being, the traits of your divine personality, what you really are and what you are meant to be.

One who has thus known himself and possessed himself, conquering all opposition within himself, has by that very fact extended himself and his conquest, making it easier for others to make the same or a similar conquest. These are the pioneers or the elite who by a victorious campaign within themselves help others towards their victory.

THE MOTHER

Here, it is written: "Our one objective must be the Divine himself to whom, knowingly or unknowingly, something always aspires in our secret nature." What is this something which aspires?

It is a part of the being which is not always the same in everyone, and which is instinctively open to the influence of the psychic.

There is always one part – sometimes indeed quite veiled, of which we are not conscious – something in the being which is turned to the psychic and receiving its influence. This is the intermediary between the psychic consciousness and the external consciousness.

It is not the same thing in everyone; in each one it is

different. It is the point in his nature or character through which he can touch the psychic and where he can receive the psychic influence. It depends upon people; for each one it is different; everyone has a point like this.

You may also feel that there are certain things which suddenly push you, lift you above yourself, open a kind of door upon something greater. It can be many things; and it depends upon each one's nature. It's the part of the being which enthuses over something; it is this capacity for enthusiasm.

There are two principal things. This, the capacity for enthusiasm which makes one come out of his greater or lesser inertia in order to throw himself more or less totally into the thing which rouses him. As for instance, the artist for his art, the scientist for his science. And in general, every person who creates or builds has an opening, the opening of a special faculty, a special possibility, creating an enthusiasm in him. When this is active, something in the being awakens, and there is a participation of almost the whole being in the thing done.

There is this. And then there are those who have an innate faculty of gratitude, those who have an ardent need to respond, respond with warmth, devotion, joy, to something which they feel like a marvel hidden behind the whole of life, behind the tiniest little element, the least little event of life, who feel this sovereign beauty or infinite Grace which is behind all things.

I knew people who had no knowledge, so to say, of anything, who were hardly educated, whose minds were altogether of the ordinary kind, and who had in them this capacity of gratitude, of warmth, which gives itself, understands and is thankful.

Well, for them, the contact with the psychic was very frequent, almost constant and, to the extent that they were capable of it, conscious – not very conscious but a little – in the sense that they felt that they were carried, helped, uplifted above themselves.

These two things prepare people the most. They are born with one or the other; and if they take the trouble, it develops gradually, it increases.

We say: the capacity for enthusiasm, something which throws you out of your miserable and mean little ego; and the generous gratitude, the generosity of the gratitude which also flings itself in thanksgiving out of the little ego. These are the two most powerful levers to enter into contact with the Divine in one's psychic being. This serves as a link with the psychic being – the surest link.

THE MOTHER

Mother, since in each new life the mind and vital as well as the body are new, how can the experiences of past lives be useful for them? Do we have to go through all the experiences once again?

That depends on people!

It is not the mind and vital which develop and progress from life to life – except in altogether exceptional cases and at a very advanced stage of evolution – it is the psychic. So, this is what happens: the psychic has alternate periods of activity and rest; it has a life of progress resulting from experiences of the physical life, of active life in a physical body, with all the experiences of the body, the vital and the mind; then, normally, the psychic goes into a kind of rest for assimilation where the result of the progress accomplished during its active existence is worked out, and when this assimilation is finished, when it has absorbed the progress it had prepared in its active life on earth, it comes down again in a new body bringing with it the result of all its progress and, at an advanced stage, it even chooses the environment and the kind of body and the kind of life in which it will live to complete its experience concerning one point or another. In some very advanced cases the psychic can, before leaving the body, decide what kind of life it will have in its next incarnation.

When it has become an almost completely formed and already very conscious being, it presides over the formation of the new body, and usually through an inner influence it chooses the elements and the substance which will form its body in such a way that the body is adapted to the needs of its new experience. But this is at a rather advanced stage. And later, when it is fully formed and returns to earth with the idea of service, of collective help and participation in the divine Work, then it is able to bring to the body in formation certain elements of the mind and vital from previous lives which, having been organised and impregnated with psychic forces in previous lives, could be preserved and, consequently, can participate in the general progress. But this is at a very, very advanced stage.

When the psychic is fully developed and very conscious, when it becomes a conscious instrument of the divine Will, it organises the vital and the mind in such a way that they too participate in the general harmony and can be preserved.

A high degree of development allows at least some

parts of the mental and vital beings to be preserved in spite of the dissolution of the body. If, for instance, some parts – mental or vital – of the human activity have been particularly developed, these elements of the mind and vital are maintained even "in their form" in the form of the activity which has been fully organised – as, for example, in highly intellectual people who have particularly developed their brains, the mental part of their being keeps this structure and is preserved in the form of an organised brain which has its own life and can be kept unchanged until a future life so as to participate in it with all its gains.

In artists, as for instance in certain musicians who have used their hands in a particularly conscious way, the vital and mental substance is preserved in the form of hands, and these hands remain fully conscious, they can even use the body of living people if there is a special affinity – and so on.

Otherwise, in ordinary people in whom the psychic form is not fully developed and organised, when the psychic leaves the body, the mental and vital forms may persist for a certain time if the death has been particularly peaceful and concentrated, but if a man dies suddenly and in a state of passion, with numerous attachments, well, the different parts of the being are dispersed and live for a shorter or longer time their own life in their own domain, then disappear.

The centre of organisation and transformation is always the presence of the psychic in the body. Therefore, it is a very big mistake to believe that the progress continues or even, as some believe, that it is more complete and rapid in the periods of transition between two physical lives; in general, there is no progress at all, for the psychic enters into a state of rest and the other parts, after a more or less ephemeral life in their own domain, are dissolved.

Earthly life is the place for progress. It is here, on earth, that progress is possible, during the period of earthly existence. And it is the psychic which carries the progress over from one life to another, by organising its own evolution and development itself.

THE MOTHER

If it is not the mind, vital or physical which take birth again but only the psychic being, then the vital or mental progress made before is of no value in another life?

It happens only to the extent the progress of these parts has brought them close to the psychic, that is, to the extent the progress lies in putting all the parts of the being successively under the psychic influence. For all that is under the psychic influence and identified with the psychic continues, and it is that alone which continues. But if the psychic is made the centre of one's life and consciousness, and if the whole being is organised around it, the whole being passes under the psychic influence, becomes united with it, and can continue – if it is necessary for it to continue.

THE MOTHER

Then everybody is progressing, always, isn't that so?

In a certain way, yes. Only it may not be apparent in one lifetime, because when there is no conscious participation of the being, the movement is relatively slow, even relative to the short duration of human life. And so it is quite possible, for example, that at the moment of death a being seems not to have progressed, and even sometimes it seems to have been going backwards, to have lost what it had at the beginning of its life. But if we take the great life-curve of its psychic being through many lives, there is always a progress. Each experience it had in one of its physical lifetimes helps it to make some progress. But it is the psychic being which always progresses.

The physical being, in the state in which it is at present – well, having reached a certain point of ascent, it comes down again. There are elements which may not come down again grossly; but still it does come down, one can't deny it.

The vital being – not necessarily, nor the mental being. The vital being, if it knows how to get connected with the universal force, can very easily have no retrogression; it can continue to ascend. And the mental being, it's absolutely certain, is completely free from all degeneration if it continues to develop normally. So these always make progress so long as they remain co-ordinated and under the influence of the psychic.

THE MOTHER

How can one make one's psychic personality grow?

It is through all the experiences of life that the psychic personality forms, grows, develops and finally becomes a complete, conscious and free being.

This process of development goes on tirelessly through innumerable lives, and if one is not conscious of it, it is because one is not conscious of one's psychic being – for that is the indispensable starting-point. Through interiorisation and concentration one has to enter into conscious contact with one's psychic being. This psychic being always has an influence on the outer being, but that influence is almost always occult, neither seen nor perceived nor felt, save on truly exceptional occasions.

In order to strengthen the contact and aid, if possible, the development of the conscious psychic personality, one should, while concentrating, turn towards it, aspire to know it and feel it, open oneself to receive its influence, and take great care, each time that one receives an indication from it, to follow it very scrupulously and sincerely. To live in a great aspiration, to take care to become inwardly calm and remain so always as far as possible, to cultivate a perfect sincerity in all the activities of one's being – these are the essential conditions for the growth of the psychic being.

THE MOTHER

If you have within you a psychic being sufficiently awake to watch over you, to prepare your path, it can draw towards you things which help you, draw people, books, circumstances, all sorts of little coincidences which come to you as though brought by some benevolent will and give you an indication, a help, a support to take decisions and turn you in the right direction. But once you have taken this decision, once you have decided to find the truth of your being, once you start sincerely on the road, then everything seems to conspire to help you to advance....

THE MOTHER

... till the self-giving is firmly psychic there will be disturbances, the interval of dark moments between bright ones. It is only the psychic that keeps on progressing in an unbroken line, its movement a continuous ascension. All other movements are broken and discontinuous. And it is not till the psychic is felt as yourself that you can be an individual even; for it is the true self in you. Before the true self is known, you are a public place, not a being. There are so many clashing forces working in you; hence, if you wish to make real progress, know your own being...

You must learn to unite what you call your individual self with your true psychic individuality. Your present individuality is a very mixed thing, a series of changes which yet preserves a certain continuity, a certain sameness or identity of vibration in the midst of all flux. It is almost like a river which is never the same and yet has a certain definiteness and persistence of its own. Your normal self is merely a shadow of your true individuality which you will realise only when this normal individual which is differently poised at different times, now in the mental, then in the vital, at other times in the physical, gets into contact with the psychic and feels it as its real being. Then you will be one, nothing will shake or disturb you, you will make steady and lasting progress...

THE MOTHER

IX

REVERSAL OF CONSCIOUSNESS
THE NEW BIRTH

A vision lightened on the viewless heights,
A wisdom illumined from the voiceless depths:
A deeper interpretation greatened Truth,
A grand reversal of the Night and Day;
All the world's values changed heightening life's aim;
A wiser word, a larger thought came in
Than what the slow labour of human mind can bring,
A secret sense awoke that could perceive
A Presence and a Greatness everywhere.
The universe was not now this senseless whirl
Borne round inert on an immense machine;
It cast away its grandiose lifeless front,
A mechanism no more or work of Chance,
But a living movement of the body of God.

SRI AUROBINDO

REVERSAL OF CONSCIOUSNESS
THE NEW BIRTH

To live the spiritual life, a reversal of consciousness is needed.... To live the spiritual life is to open to another world within oneself. It is to reverse one's consciousness, as it were. The ordinary human consciousness, even in the most developed, even in men of great talent and great realisation, is a movement turned outwards – all the energies are directed outwards, the whole consciousness is spread outwards; and if anything is turned inwards, it is very little, very rare, very fragmentary, it happens only under the pressure of very special circumstances, violent shocks, the shocks life gives precisely with the intention of slightly reversing this movement of exteriorisation of the consciousness.

But all who have lived a spiritual life have had the same experience: all of a sudden something in their being has been reversed, so to speak, has been turned suddenly and sometimes completely inwards, and also at the same time upwards, from within upwards – but it is not an external "above", it is within, deep, something other than the heights as they are physically conceived. Something has literally been turned over. There has been a decisive experience and the standpoint in life, the way of looking at life, the attitude one takes in relation to it, has suddenly changed, and in some cases quite definitively, irrevocably.

... so long as one is in the mental consciousness, even the highest, and sees the spiritual life from outside, one judges with one's mental faculties, with the habit of seeking, erring, correcting, progressing, and seeking once again; and one thinks that those who are in the spiritual life suffer from the same incapacity, but that is a very gross mistake!

When the reversal of the being has taken place, all that is finished. One no longer seeks, one sees. One no longer deduces, one knows. One no longer gropes, one walks straight to the goal.

THE MOTHER

"... we have only accomplished weakness and effort and a defeated victory...."

SRI AUROBINDO

(*Thoughts and Glimpses*, Centenary Library, Vol. 16, p. 379)

Through a very assiduous labour one succeeds in overcoming a weakness, a limitation, a bad habit, and one believes this is a definitive victory; but after some time or at times immediately one realises that nothing is completely done, nothing is definitive, that what one thought to have accomplished has to be done again. For only a total change of consciousness and the intervention of a new force, a reversal of consciousness can make the victory complete.

In the old Chaldean tradition, very often the young novices were given an image when they were invested with the white robe; they were told: "Do not try to remove the stains one by one, the whole robe must be purified." Do not try to correct your faults one by one, to overcome your weaknesses one by one, it does not take you very far. The entire consciousness must be changed, a reversal of consciousness must be achieved, a springing up out of the state in which one is towards a higher state from which one dominates all the weaknesses one wants to heal, and from which one has a full vision of the work to be accomplished.

I believe Sri Aurobindo has said this: things are such that it may be said that nothing is done until everything is done. One step ahead is not enough, a total conversion is necessary.

How many times have I heard people who were making an effort say, "I try, but what's the use of my trying? Every time I think I have gained something, I find that I must begin all over again." This happens because they are trying to go forward while standing still, they are trying to progress without changing their consciousness. It is the entire point of view which must be shifted, the whole consciousness must get out of the rut in which it lies so as to rise up and see things from above. It is only thus that victories will not be changed into defeats.

THE MOTHER

There is one phenomenon which obviously seems indispensable if one wants the realisation to become stable.... Experiences come, touch the consciousness, sometimes bring great illuminations, then get blurred, retreat into the background and, outwardly, in your ordinary consciousness, you don't feel that there is a great change, a great difference. And this phenomenon may occur very often, may repeat itself for many years. Suddenly you get a sort of revelation, like an illumination, you are in the true consciousness and have the feeling of having got hold of the real thing. And then, slowly or suddenly, it seems to

recede behind you, and you seek but do not find that there
is any great change in you.... These things seem to come
as heralds or as promises: "See, it will happen", or to tell
you, "Well, have faith, it *will be* like that."

And this may recur very often. There is progress,
obviously, but it is very slow and hardly apparent.

But then, suddenly – perhaps because one is sufficiently
prepared, perhaps simply because the time has come, and
it has been so decreed – suddenly, when such an experience occurs, its result in the part of the being where it
takes place is a complete reversal of consciousness. It is a
very clear, very concrete phenomenon. The best way of
describing it is this: a complete reversal. And then the
relation of the consciousness with the other parts of the
being and with the outer world is as if completely changed.
Absolutely like an overturning. And that reversal no
longer comes back to the same old place, the consciousness no longer returns to its former position – Sri
Aurobindo would say "status". Once this has happened
in any part of the being, this part of the being is
stabilised.

And until that happens, it comes and goes, comes and
goes, one advances and then has the impression of
marking time, and one advances again and then marks
time again, and sometimes one feels as though one were
going backwards, and it is interminable – and indeed it is
interminable. It may last for years and years and years.
But when this reversal of consciousness takes place,
whether in the mind or a part of the mind, whether in the
vital or a part of the vital, or even in the physical
consciousness itself and in the body-consciousness, once
this is established, it is over; you no longer go back, you

do not ever return to what you were before. And this is the true indication that you have taken a step forward definitively. And before this, there are only preparations.

Those who have experienced this reversal know what I am speaking about; but if one hasn't, one can't understand. One may have a kind of idea by analogy, people who have tried to describe yoga compare it with the reversal of a prism: when you put it at a certain angle, the light is white; when you turn it over, it is broken up. Well, this is exactly what happens, that is to say, you restore the white. In the ordinary consciousness there is decomposition and you restore the white. However, this is only an image. It is not really *that*, this is an analogy. But the phenomenon is extremely concrete. It is almost as though you were to put what is inside out, and what is outside in. And it isn't that either! But if you could turn a ball inside-out, or a balloon – you can't, can you? – if you could put the inside out and the outside in, it would be something like what I mean.

And one can't say that one "experiences" this reversal – there is no "feeling", it is almost a mechanical fact – it is extraordinarily mechanical. (*Mother takes an object from the table beside her and turns it upside down....*) There would be some very interesting things to say about the difference between the moment of realisation, of *siddhi* – like this reversal of consciousness for example – and all the work of development, the *tapasyā*; to say how it comes about.... For the sadhana, *tapasyā* is one thing and the *siddhi* another, quite a different thing. You may do *tapasyā* for centuries, and you will always go as at a tangent – closer and closer to the realisation, nearer and nearer, but it is only when the *siddhi* is given to you... then, everything is changed, everything is reversed. And this is inexpressible, for as soon as it is put in words it escapes. But there is a difference – a real difference, essential, total – between aspiration, the mental tension, even the tension of the highest, most luminous mind and realisation: something which has been decided above from all time and is absolutely independent of all personal effort, of all gradation. Don't you see, it is not bit by bit that one reaches it, it is not by a small, constant, regular effort, it is not that: it is something that comes suddenly; it is established without one's knowing how or why, but all is changed.

And it will be like that for everybody, for the whole universe: it goes on and on, it moves forward very slowly, and then one moment, all of a sudden, *it will be done*, finished – not finished: it's the beginning!

THE MOTHER

This change of consciousness and its preparation have often been compared with the formation of the chicken in the egg: till the very last second the egg remains the same, there is no change, and it is only when the chicken is completely formed, absolutely alive, that it itself makes with its little beak a hole in the shell and comes out. Something similar takes place at the moment of the change of consciousness. For a long time you have the impression that nothing is happening, that your consciousness is the same as usual, and, if you have an intense aspiration, you even feel a resistance, as though you were knocking against a wall which does not yield. But when you are ready within, a last effort – the pecking in the shell of the being – and everything opens and you are projected into another consciousness.

I said that it was a revolution of the basic equilibrium, that is, a total reversal of consciousness comparable with what happens to light when it passes through a prism. Or it is as though you were turning a ball inside out, which cannot be done except in the fourth dimension. One comes out of the ordinary three-dimensional consciousness to enter the higher four-dimensional consciousness, and into an infinite number of dimensions. This is the indispensable starting-point. Unless your consciousness changes its dimension, it will remain just what it is with the superficial vision of things, and all the profundities will escape you.

THE MOTHER

What is called "new birth" is the birth into the spiritual life, the spiritual consciousness; it is to carry in oneself something of the spirit which, individually, through the soul, can begin to rule the life and be the master of existence....

In the individual existence, that is what makes all the difference; so long as one just speaks of the spirit and it is something one has read about, whose existence one vaguely knows about, but not a very concrete reality for the consciousness, this means that one is not born into the spirit. And when one is born into the spirit, it becomes something much more concrete, much more living, much more real, much more tangible than the whole material world. And this is what makes the essential difference between beings. When *that* becomes spontaneously real –

the true, concrete existence, the atmosphere one can freely breathe – then one knows one has crossed over to the other side. But so long as it is something rather vague and hazy – you have heard about it, you know that it exists, but... it has no concrete reality – well, this means that the new birth has not yet taken place. As long as you tell yourself, "Yes, this I can see, this I can touch, the pain I suffer from, the hunger that torments me, the sleep that makes me feel heavy, this is real, this is concrete..." (*Mother laughs*), that means that you have not yet crossed over to the other side, you are not born into the spirit.

THE MOTHER

> *Is it possible to change this at once, change this consciousness?... One feels that it will be a revolution to change that.*

Yes, but a revolution can occur in half a second; it can also take years, even centuries, and even many lives. It can be done in a second.

One can do it. Precisely, when one has this inner reversal of consciousness, in one second everything, everything changes... precisely this bewilderment of being able to think that what one is, what one considers as oneself is not true, and that what is the truth of one's being is something one doesn't know. You see, this should have been the normal reaction, the one she had, of saying, "But then what is myself? If what I feel as myself is an illusory formation and not the truth of my being, then what is myself?" For that she doesn't know. And so when one asks the question like that...

There is a moment – because it is a question which becomes more and more intense and more and more acute – when you have even the feeling, precisely, that things are strange, that is, they are not real; a moment comes when this sensation that you have of yourself, of being yourself, becomes strange, a kind of sense of unreality. And the question continues coming up: "But then what is myself?" Well, there is a moment when it comes up with so much concentration and such intensity that with this intensity of concentration suddenly there occurs a reversal, and then instead of being on this side you are on that side, and when you are on that side everything is very simple; you understand, you know, you are, you live, and then you see clearly the unreality of the rest, and this is enough.

You see, one may have to wait for days, months, years, centuries, lives, before this moment comes. But if one intensifies his aspiration, there is a moment when the pressure is so great and the intensity of the question so strong that something turns over in the consciousness, and then this is absolutely what one feels: instead of being here one is there, instead of seeing from outside and seeking to see within, one is inside; and the minute one is within, absolutely everything changes, completely, and all that seemed to him true, natural, normal, real, tangible, all that, immediately, – yes, it seems to him very grotesque, very queer, very unreal, quite absurd; but one has touched something which is supremely true and eternally beautiful, and this one never loses again.

Once the reversal has taken place, you can glide into an external consciousness, not lose the ordinary contact with the things of life, but that remains and it never moves.

You may, in your dealings with others, fall back a little into their ignorance and blindness, but there is always something there, living, standing up within, which does not move any more, until it manages to penetrate everything, to the point where it is over, where the blindness disappears for ever. And this is an absolutely tangible experience, something more concrete than the most concrete object, more concrete than a blow on your head, something more real than anything whatever.

THE MOTHER

... so long as there is any doubt or hesitation, so long as one asks oneself the question of whether one has or hasn't realised this eternal soul in oneself, it proves that the *true* contact has not taken place. For, when the phenomenon occurs, it brings with it an inexpressible something, so new and so definitive, that doubt and questioning are no longer possible. It is truly, in the absolute sense of the phrase, a new birth.

You become a new person, and whatever may be the path or the difficulties of the path afterwards, that feeling never leaves you. It is not even something – like many other experiences – which withdraws, passes into the background, leaving you externally with a kind of vague memory to which it is difficult to cling, whose remembrance grows faint, blurred – it is not that. You *are* a new person and definitively that, whatever happens. And even all the incapacity of the mind, all the difficulties of the vital, all the inertia of the physical are unable to change this new state – a new state which makes a *decisive* break in the life of the consciousness. The being one was before and the being one is after, are no longer the same. The position one has in the universe and in relation to it, in life and in relation to it, in understanding and in relation to it, is no longer the same: it is a true reversal which can never be undone again.

THE MOTHER

... these are not words, it is altogether true that *everything* changes its appearance, totally, that life and things are completely different from what they appear to be.

All this contact, this ordinary perception of the world loses its reality completely. This is what appears unreal, fantastic, illusory, non-existent. There is something – something very material, very concrete, very physical – which becomes the reality of the being, and which has nothing in common with the ordinary way of seeing. When one has this perception – the perception of the work of the divine force, of the movement being worked out behind the appearance, *in* the appearance, through the appearance – one begins to be ready to live something truer than the ordinary human falsehood. But not before.

There is no compromise, you see. It is not like a convalescence after an illness: you must change worlds. So long as your mind is real for you, your way of thinking something true for you, real, concrete, it proves that you are not there yet. You must first pass through to the other side. Afterwards you will be able to understand what I am telling you.

Pass through to the other side.

It is not true that one can understand little by little, it is not like that. This kind of progress is different. What is more true is that one is shut up in a shell, and inside it something is happening, like the chick in the egg. It is getting ready in there. It is in there. One doesn't see it. Something is happening in the shell, but outside one sees nothing. And it is only when all is ready that there comes the capacity to pierce the shell and to be born into the light of day.

It is not that one becomes more and more perceptible or visible: one is shut in – shut in – and for sensitive people there is even that terrible sensation of being compressed, of trying to pass through and then coming up against a wall. And then one knocks and knocks and knocks, and one can't go through.

And so long as one is there, inside, one is in the falsehood. And only on the day when by the Divine Grace one can break the shell and come out into the Light, is one free.

This may happen suddenly, spontaneously, quite unexpectedly.

I don't think one can go through gradually. I don't think it is something which slowly wears and wears away until one can see through it. I haven't had an instance of this so far. There is rather a kind of accumulation of power inside, an intensification of the need, and an endurance in the effort which becomes free from all fear, all anxiety, all calculation; a need so imperative that one no longer cares for the consequences.

One is like an explosive that nothing can resist, and one bursts out from one's prison in a blaze of light.

After that one can no longer fall back again.

It is truly a new birth.

THE MOTHER

GLOSSARY

(Most of the explanations given below are based on Sri Aurobindo's writings. Some of the terms may have a different meaning in another context; explanations given below have generally been limited to the context in which the terms occur in this book.)

ādhār (Adhar)

vehicle, vessel or support; that in which the consciousness is now contained – mind-life-body.

adhikārī

one who, by virtue of capacity, has a right to a particular way of yoga.

agni (Agni)

fire; the godhead of fire.

ānandā (Ananda)

bliss, delight, beatitude, spiritual ecstasy; a self-delight which is the very nature of the transcendent and infinite existence.

aprakāśa

absence of light: obscurity, forgetfulness.

apravṛtti

non-action; inertia.

āsana (Asana)

[in Hathayoga]: posture.

ātman (Atman)

Self; Spirit; the original and essential nature of Existence or Being.

Asuric

pertaining to *asura*, a hostile being or force of the vital mental plane, known in traditional Indian legends as the dark Titan or demon.

avatāra (Avatar)

Incarnation; the Divine manifest in a human form.

Being

the Self; the sole and fundamental Reality or Truth of existence; all that exists is part of the one indivisible Being.

The One Being manifests itself on different planes or levels of consciousness, and in the individual being is constituted by different distinguishable parts of the indivisible Being.

The part of our nature of which we are normally conscious is our surface or outer being consisting of the body, the (surface) vital (related to life-energy and emotions, desires, passions, etc.), and the (surface) mind (having to do with cognition, intelligence, ideas, thought perceptions, etc.).

Behind this superficial consciousness there exists a far greater, deeper and more powerful consciousness in touch with the universal planes of Mind, Life and Matter. This hidden consciousness, referred to as our inner or true being, consists of the true or inner mental, the true or inner vital and the true or inner physical, with the psychic (the soul) as the innermost being which, as an aspect of the central being, supports all the different parts in the manifestation and which develops over the course of evolution an individuality which is called the psychic being.

The inner being is also sometimes referred to as the subliminal (being) or subliminal consciousness. It opens above to the Superconscient and below to the Subconscient and the Inconscient.

bhakti (Bhakti)

love for the Divine; devotion to the Divine.

bhaktiyoga

the yoga (path) of devotion.

bhoga

enjoyment, possession.

Brahman
> the Reality; the Absolute; the Spirit; the Supreme Being; the One besides whom there is nothing else existent.

Central Being
> the portion of the Divine which supports the individual being and survives from life to life; it has two forms: *jīvātman*, which is above the manifestation in life, presiding over it, and the psychic beng, which stands behind mind, life and body in the manifestation, supporting them and using them as its instruments.

citta
> basic consciousness; the general stuff of mixed mental-vital-physical consciousness out of which arise the movements of thought, emotion, sensation, impulse, etc.

Concentration
> a gathering together of the consciousness, either centralizing at one inner or outer object; there can also be a gathered condition throughout the being, not at a point.

Consciousness
> the Force aspect of Being; whose energy and movement creates the universe and all that is in it; it is made up of two elements: awareness of self and things, and conscious force.

Contemplation
> a form of meditation; mentally regarding a single object, image or idea so that the knowledge about the object, image or idea may arise naturally in the mind by force of the concentration.

Cosmic
> of the cosmos; universal. (*cf.* Transcendent)

the Dhammapada
> a Buddhist scripture containing teachings of the Buddha.

the Divine
the Supreme Truth or Being.

Ego
the "I" constituted by a mental, vital and physical formation which serves to centralise and individualise the outer consciousness and action; when the true self is discovered, the utility of the ego ceases, this formation disappears and the true individuality is felt in its place; *see also* Individuality.

Equality
equal-mindedness.

Evolution
the process by which the One Being and Consciousness, involved in Matter and Inconscience, progressively liberates itself, evolving from Matter into Life, from Life into Mind, from Mind into the Spirit.

Experience (spiritual)
inner happening in the spiritual life when the veil of the outer being begins to be lifted; *see also* Realization.

the Gita
an episode in the ancient epic *Mahabharata* in which, on the battlefield of Kurukshetra, the Divine, in the form of Sri Krishna, gives his teachings to Arjuna.

Guru
spiritual teacher, guide.

Higher Consciousness
see Superconscient.

the Inconscient
the most involved state of the Superconscience; all powers of the Superconscience progressively evolve and emerge out of the Inconscient, the first emergence being Matter.

Individuality

    essential or true I-ness which is one with all Being, as distinguished from the false I-ness of the ego which is felt as separate from everyone and everything else.

Inner being

    see Being.

Inner Consciousness

    see Being.

Integral Yoga

    Sri Aurobindo's yoga which aims at attaining the supramental consciousness and bringing it down to transform mind, life and body.

Involution

    the process of downward evolution by which the Supreme Consciousness reaches the opposite pole of Inconscience out of which all evolves upwards.

Ishta Devata

    the chosen deity; the special name, form, idea of Divinity which each man may choose for worship and communion.

japa

    repetition of a sacred syllable, name or mystic formula called a *mantra*.

kāla

    Time (in its essentiality).

Karmayoga

    the yoga path of works.

kṣaya

    loss, waste.

Life

    Life-Force; the vital being or vital plane of consciousness (between Matter and Mind).

Mara

in Buddhism: the Destroyer, the Evil One (who tempts man to indulge his passions); conscious devil or self-existent principle of evil.

māyā (Maya)

the power of self-illusion in Brahman; illusion.

Meditation

the concentration of the mind on a single train of ideas which work out a single subject; as a general term it includes many other kinds of inner activity such as detached observation of inner movements, self-opening and receptivity to what may come from a higher state of consciousness, dwelling on a lofty idea or state (the Divine, peace, etc.); meditation is generally diffusive in contrast to concentration.

Mind (the mental)

see Being.

Nature

see prakṛti (Prakriti).

Occult

pertaining to the knowledge or existence of supernatural agencies, realities and influences capable of impinging upon, but hidden from, gross physical nature.

Overmind

the highest of the planes of consciousness below the Supramental; *see* Being.

prakṛti (Prakriti)

Nature; Nature-Force. "Existence is composed of Prakriti and Purusha, the consciousness that sees and the consciousness that executes and formalises what we see. The one we call Soul, the other Nature." (Sri Aurobindo); *see also puruṣa* (Purusha).

Psyche (the psychic)
   spark of the Divine before it has evolved into an individualised
   being; *see also* Psychic Being.

Psychic Being
   the soul; when the psyche, a spark of the Divine, present in all
   life and matter begins to develop an individuality in the course
   of evolution, that psychic individuality is called the psychic
   being; *see also* Being.

puruṣa (Purusha)
   Conscious Being; Conscious-Soul; essential being supporting
   the play of *prakṛti*; the Purusha represents the true being on
   whatever plane it manifests – physical, vital, mental, psychic.

Rajayoga
   a system of yoga, taught by Patanjali, which uses the mental
   askesis for the opening of the divine life on all its planes.

Rajayogi
   one who practises Rajayoga.

Rajasic
   dominantly characterized by *rajas*, the quality of passion or
   drive of propensity.

Realization
   attainment of the higher consciousness; inner happenings in
   the spiritual life are called experiences when they come about
   in flashes, snatches or rare visitations, and are spoken of as
   realizations when they become positive, frequent or normal.

Rishi
   a seer.

Sadhak, Sadhaka
   a practitioner of yoga.

Sadhana
   the practice of yoga.

Samadhi
> yogic trance (in which the mind acquires the capacity of withdrawing from its limited waking activities into freer and higher states of consciousness).

samatā
> equality; equanimity; the state in which one remains unmoved within under all conditions.

śāstra (Shastra)
> any systematized teaching and science.

Sattwic
> dominantly characterized by *sattva*, the quality of poise, peace and knowledge.

Shastra
> see *śāstra*.

Siddhi
> perfection or fulfilment in yoga.

the Subconscient
> *see* Being.

the Subliminal
> *see* Being.

Subtle physical
> the plane closest to the physical.

śuddhā bhakti
> pure love or devotion for the Divine.

Supramental Consciousness (the Supramental)
> Truth-Consciousness; the highest plane of consciousness above and beyond the mind.

Tamasic
> dominantly characterized by *tamas*, the quality of inertia and ignorance.

tapasyā
  effort or austerity of the personal will for self-control or self-transformation.

the Transcendent
  above and beyond the cosmic manifestation; the Transcendent, the Universal (Cosmic) and the Individual are three aspects of Being pervading the whole manifestation.

Transformation
  bringing down the higher consciousness into the mental, vital .and physical consciousness; in Sri Aurobindo's yoga the term connotes specifically the radical change brought about in mind, vital and body by the descent of the highest – the Supramental-consciousness – into these parts.

Tratak
  concentration of the vision on a single point or object, generally a luminous object.

the Universal
  cosmic; *see* the Transcendent.

Upanishads
  a class of Hindu sacred writings, regarded as the source of the Vedanta philosophy.

utsāha
  zeal; the force of one's personal effort.

Veda
  generic name for the most ancient Indian sacred literature; knowledge; the book of knowledge.

vijñāna
  the comprehensive aspect of the true unifying knowledge; the pure perception of Truth; Gnosis.

the Vital (being)
  see Being.

vyākulatā
the heart's eagerness for the attainment of the Divine.

Yoga
the discipline by which one seeks consciously and deliberately
to realise union with the Divine or, more generally, to attain a
higher consciousness.

yoga-siddhi
the perfection which comes by the practice of yoga.

yogin (Yogi)
one who practises yoga; one who is established in spiritual
realisation.

REFERENCES

The passages in this book have been selected from the following volumes of Sri Aurobindo Birth Centenary Library and the Collected Works of the Mother, published by the Sri Aurobindo Ashram, Pondicherry.

SRI AUROBINDO BIRTH CENTENARY LIBRARY

Volume	Title
16	The Supramental Manifestation & Other Writings
18	The Life Divine: Book One and Book Two, Part One
19	The Life Divine: Book Two, Part Two
20	The Synthesis of Yoga: Parts One and Two
22	Letters on Yoga: Part One
23	Letters on Yoga: Parts Two and Three
24	Letters on Yoga: Part Four
28	Savitri: Part One

COLLECTED WORKS OF THE MOTHER

Volume	Title
3	Questions and Answers
4	Questions and Answers 1950-51
5	Questions and Answers 1953
6	Questions and Answers 1954
7	Questions and Answers 1955
8	Questions and Answers 1956
9	Questions and Answers 1957-58
10	On Thoughts and Aphorisms
12	On Education
14	Words of the Mother
15	Words of the Mother
16	Some Answers from the Mother

All the extracts from the writings of Sri Aurobindo are in English; those of the Mother are either in English or translated into English from the French original.

The references below are given in an abbreviated form. A number set in **boldface type** indicates the page number of this book on which a given passage begins. The number which follows, if prefixed by SA, indicates the volume number of Sri Aurobindo Birth Centenary Library; if prefixed by MO, it refers to the volume number of the Collected Works of the Mother. The subsequent numbers are the pages of the particular volume from which the passage has been extracted. For example, **2a.** SA20:430 means that the first passage on page 2 of this book is taken from volume 20 of Sri Aurobindo Birth Centenary Library, page 430.

The references follow:

2a. SA20:430. **2b.** SA19:843. **3.** MO9:261-63. **5.** MO9:45-46. **7.** MO8:367-68. **8.** MO8:368-69. **9a.** MO10:297. **9b.** MO9:15-19. **13.** MO3:1-2. **14a.** MO4:36. **14b.** SA19:694. **16a.** SA19:857. **16b.** SA16:15. **17.** SA20:63-65. **20.** MO4:255. **21.** MO6:421-23. **22.** MO9:373-75. **24.** MO8:402-05. **27a.** MO9:373-74. **27b.** MO4:103. **28.** MO9:419-21. **32a.** SA20:47. **32b.** SA23:576. **32c.** SA23:560. **32d.** MO8:400. **33.** SA20:51-52. **34a.** MO8:252. **34b.** MO4:67-68. **36.** MO5:141-45. **38a.** MO8:248-49. **38b.** SA23:560. **39a.** SA23:561. **39b.** MO6:397-98. **41a.** MO9:119. **41b.** SA23:572-73. **42.** SA23:616. **43.** MO3:189. **44.** MO6:440-41. **45a.** MO9:352. **45b.** SA20:48-50. **49.** MO7:213-15. **51.** MO6:350-51. **52.** SA20:58-60. **54.** SA20:60-61. **55a.** MO14:61. **55b.** MO14:61. **56a.** SA23:617. **56b.** SA23:624. **57a.** SA23:627. **57b.** SA23:630. **57c.** SA23:625. **57d.** SA23:623. **57e.** SA23:623. **58.** SA23:650-51. **59.** MO9:316-17. **60a.** MO14:177. **60b.** SA24:1632. **60c.** SA24:1358-59. **62a.** SA23:574-75. **62b.** SA23:656. **63.** SA20:295. **64a.** SA23:886. **64b.** MO6:438-40. **66.** MO4:360. **67.** MO5:214-15. **68.** SA20:303. **69a.** SA20:308-09. **69b.** MO9:360-61. **70.** SA23:517. **71a.** MO16:180. **71b.** MO16:180. **72a.** SA23:661-62. **72b.** SA23:641. **73a.** SA23:642-43. **73b.** SA23:649. **73c.** SA23:656. **73d.** SA23:651. **74a.** SA23:650. **74b.** SA23:644. **74c.** SA23:644. **74d.** SA23:654. **75a.** SA23:641. **75b.** SA23:738. **75c.** MO8:329-31. **78.** MO6:313-14. **82a.** SA23:532. **82b.** MO12:4-5. **83.** MO15:324-25. **84a.** SA23:526. **84b.** SA23:526. **84c.** SA23:536. **85.** SA23:721-22. **86.** SA23:722-23. **87a.** SA23:727-28. **87b.** MO8:88-89. **89a.** SA23:729. **89b.** SA23:723. **90a.** SA23:723. **90b.** SA23:723-25. **91a.** SA23:726. **91b.** SA23:726. **92.** SA23:731-32. **93a.** SA23:538. **93b.** SA23:530. **93c.** SA23:706. **94a.** SA23:531. **94b.** SA23:531. **94c.** SA23:528. **95a.** SA23:669. **95b.** SA23:672. **95c.** SA23:673. **96a.** SA23:674. **96b.** SA23:669. **96c.** SA23:677. **97a.** SA23:692. **97b.** SA23:679. **97c.** MO8:160-61. **99a.** SA23:680. **99b.** SA23:680-81. **99c.** SA23:535. **100a.** SA23:689-90. **100b.** SA23:691. **101a.** SA23:537. **101b.** MO14:320. **101c.** SA23:782-83. **101d.** SA23:776. **102a.** SA23:533. **102b.**

SA23:777. **102c.** SA23:780. **103a.** SA23:785. **103b.** MO8:324-25. **105.** SA23:608-09. **108.** SA24:1615. **109.** SA24:1618-19. **111a.** SA24:1640. **111b.** SA24:1641-42. **112.** SA24:1648-49. **113.** SA24:1653-54. **114.** MO4:179-81. **116.** MO3:43. **117.** MO6:16-17. **119a.** MO3:6-7. **119b.** SA23:569. **120a.** SA23:908. **120b.** SA23:910. **121a.** SA23:909-10. **121b.** SA24:1672. **122.** SA19:905-06. **124.** SA23:912. **126a.** SA23:884-85. **126b.** SA23:1004. **127.** MO6:351-55. **132.** SA23:625-26. **133.** SA23:878. **134.** SA23:887-88. **135a.** SA23:1021. **135b.** SA23:1052-53. **136.** SA23:1053. **137a.** SA23:1054. **137b.** SA23:1054. **137c.** SA23:891. **138a.** SA23:892. **138b.** SA23:906-07. **139.** SA23:1047. **140a.** SA23:1056. **140b.** SA23:1056. **140c.** SA23:1055. **141a.** SA23:1014. **141b.** SA23:925. **141c.** SA23:925-26. **142.** MO8:331-32. **143.** MO8:278-79. **144.** MO7:34-36. **148a.** SA18:610. **148b.** SA23:1020-21. **149.** SA22:438-39. **150.** MO15:355-58. **154.** MO7:422-24. **156.** MO9:268-70. **159a.** MO5:359. **159b.** MO7:425-26. **160.** MO16:223:24. **161.** MO4:261. **162.** MO3:124-25. **164.** SA28:42. **165.** MO9:414-16. **166.** MO8:402. **167.** MO8:172-74. **170.** MO4:18-19. **171.** MO9:431. **172.** MO7:195-96. **174.** MO9:336-37. **175.** MO9:135-36.

INDEX

Aspiration   33, 34, 114, 119
   and prayer   36-37
Awakening (of conscious-
   ness)   2, 6, 8-9, 11-12,
   13, 16, 21, 25, 29
Awareness   xi-xii; *see also*
   Consciousness (awareness)

Being
   central   104 fn
   inner   xii-xiii, xv, 135, 137,
   148
   law of one's   xviii
   subliminal   xiv; *see also* Being,
   inner
   surface   vii
   truth of   14, 154, 172
Bhakti   101, 102, 103

Calm (Calmness)   72, 75, 77
Collectivity
   influence of   14
Concentration   vi, 35, 62, 68,
   69-71, 75, 85, 90, 91, 92
   and meditation   71, 89, 90
Consciousness (awareness)   3-5,
   8-9, 114-15
   and individualisation   14
   and self-mastery   4
   and yoga   13
Consciousness (state)   v-ix;
   xiv-xv, 126, 138, 171
   centres of   xv
   change of   24-26, 170
   characteristics   vi-ix
   cosmic   ix, ix fn
   dispersion of   vi-vii

evolution of   iii, v
gradations   151
inner   xii
normal   vi-ix, xii
of self   14
reversal of   v, xxi, 165, 166,
   168-69, 171, 172
supreme   xv
Contemplation   85

Desire   7
Difficulties   108, 109, 110, 111
Divine, the   xvi
   contact with   156
   personal and impersonal   xx,
   101
Dreams   xii, 132

Ego   iv, v
   and consciousness   7
   and individualisation   14
   and individuality   7
Equality (Equanimity)   ix, 62,
   64, 72, 99
Evolution   xiii-xiv
   and inner growth   iii
   conscious   iii, 2
   two modes of   iii
Experience(s)   126, 127, 129,
   132, 133, 137, 138, 142-45,
   156-57
   and change of nature   125,
   138
   and feeling   134
   and mental knowledge   49
   and mental preparation   51
   and purification   134-35

and realisation 126
eagerness for 64
intensity of 138
main forms of 133-34
speaking of 141
visions 51

Faith 41, 42, 44-45, 60
and belief 42
and difficulties 44
and experience 41-42
and knowledge 32

Gestalt therapy xii
Gita, the 47, 63, 85, 95, 109
Grace (Divine) 105-06, 117, 143
Growth
inner v-vi
inner, and awareness xii
inner, and evolution iii
inner, and moral
development xi
inner and personal ix
personal v
transpersonal v
Guru (*guru*) 47
channel of the Divine 56
surrender to 55
see also Teacher

Habits 5-6, 109

Inconscience 14, 109, 148
and desire 7
Individualisation 14
Individuality
a conquest 6
and ego 7
Integral Yoga 47, 55, 104 fn

Intermediate stage/zone 135-36,
137

Japa 102

Karmayoga 99; *see also* Works

Life-force 104 fn

Meditation 85, 88, 93
and concentration 71, 89, 90
and spiritual life xix
and work 93, 100
dynamic 88
essential conditions 86-87
posture for 87
Mind
liberation from 29
Morality xi, 65-66

Patience 56, 57, 60, 74
Peace 62, 73, 74, 75, 78-79
Personality 151
psychic 160
Prayer
and aspiration 36-37
and meditation 102
Progress 58, 59, 159, 160, 162
Psychic, the (psychic entity) xvi,
148, 154-58, 160; *see also*
Soul
Psychic being xvi, 11, 20, 25,
64, 104 fn, 139, 148, 152,
156, 157, 158, 159, 162
action of 161
and Atman 149
and emotion 102
influence of 161
see also Soul

Psychic fire   34
Purification (Purity)   xix, 62, 63,
    64-66, 67-68, 73, 74, 134-35

Quiet(ness) (Quietude)   vii, 73,
    74, 75, 77

Realisation   126
Rejection   139
Resistance   xiv, xiv fn, 110

Samadhi   141
śāstra (Shastra)   32, 47, 48
Sincerity   32, 38, 39, 65, 66
Soul, the   xvi, 148, 149, 152; *see
    also* Psychic, the *and* Psychic
    being
Spirituality   xix, 16, 65, 126
    and moral development   xi
Subliminal *see under* Being

Teacher   18, 32, 52-55; *see also*
    Guru

Unconsciousness
    emergence from   5, 8; *see also*
    Consciousness (awareness)

Vision(s)   131, 132, 134
Vivekananda   67, 83, 85

Work/s (Karmayoga)   93, 95, 96,
    99, 100, 101
    and meditation   93, 94, 100,
    101
    division of   97
    two ways of   99

Yoga   iii, x, 120, 121,
    124
    and consciousness   13
    call to   17-20
    difficulties in   110, 116; *see
        also* Difficulties
    object of   103
    of Nature   iii, iv
    of works   99; *see also* Works
        (Karmayoga)
    perils in   122-23
    process of   33
    purpose of   119
    the Gita's   95
    three supports of   84-85